Basic Disputing Certification

BASIC DISPUTING COURSE WORKBOOK

Lesson #1 **Credit Basics**

Welcome to the Basic Disputing Course! This training is a must for anyone that is serious about credit repair. My name is Corey Gray and I will be your instructor. I have over two decades of entrepreneurial credit repair experience.

I started his first credit repair company in the late 90's and have built, sold and influenced many other credit repair businesses since. My goal is to give you everything you need to start repairing credit. In order to get there, we want to make sure everyone understands what credit actually is - so we're going to start with the easy stuff here on lesson #1.

A little history lesson on the credit system and why credit is so important. We will break down the elements of what a credit report really is. We'll talk about how credit scores are calculated and how debt impacts your credit. At the end, we will share some tips on how to optimize your scores. Then afterwards we will get into a more in depth lesson on repairing credit!

What is Credit?

So, what exactly is "Credit"? In short, it is record keeping of your personal and financial information. The real definition of "Credit" is: Confidence in a purchaser's ability and intention to pay, and entrusting the buyer with goods or services without immediate payment.

In order to track all of this data, companies use credit reporting systems and credit reports. Companies use these systems and reports to decide whether or not to give you credit or a loan and how much interest their going to charge you for it. Your credit report is based on bills you have paid, missed or been late paying, loans that you have paid off, plus your current amount of debt.

A credit report contains information on where you work and live, how you pay your bills, and whether you've been sued, or filed for bankruptcy. Credit Reporting Agencies also called "Credit Bureaus" gather this information and sell it to creditors, employers, insurers, and they even sell it back to you (the consumer) in the form of credit reports and credit scores.

Credit reporting began more than 100 years ago. There is some dispute about who started it, and where, but the approach was basically the same. In the late 1800s and early 1900s several individuals in different cities began going from merchant to merchant taking notes about the people with whom they had credit arrangements. Those notes could say anything from, "He's a reliable customer and always repays the debt," to "He won't pay, but his father will cover what he owes."

When a customer would ask for credit from a merchant, the merchant would call the local credit reporter who would share the information they had on file about the person. Over time, credit reporting became purely objective and came to include only account payment history. It also grew from a local business to a major national industry. In the late 1960s, credit reporting became computerized, which made it possible to become truly national in scope. In 1970 the Fair Credit Reporting Act (FCRA) became the first law to govern consumer reporting, including credit reports.

The FCRA has been amended several times but remains the primary national law governing credit reporting. It specifies who can get a copy of your credit report, under what circumstances, and what the report can include. It also defines the responsibilities of credit reporting companies, and the responsibilities of businesses that choose to report information to credit reporting companies.

Most states also have laws that regulate credit reporting. The laws recognize that lenders need credit references to protect their businesses from losses and provide better services to their customers. By sharing credit payment information lenders are able to make better decisions and make credit available to more people and at a lower cost. And like no other reference service, consumers have full access to the information that is shared.

Why is Credit Important?

Your credit is your reputation, once you mess it up - it takes some time to rebuild it! Your credit impacts virtually every aspect of your life. (at least most people don't have cash to purchase everything, it's just the way it is) Your credit score is also a direct reflection of what risk you are and how much you'll pay in interest. If you want a home or a car, CREDIT the first thing the bank will ask about.

If you are looking for a personal loan or a BUSINESS loan, same thing... "What's your credit score?" Homeowners insurance, car insurance, even life insurance companies are now pulling your credit. Employers look at your credit, especially for jobs with any type of financial responsibility will want to see that you are financially responsible and your credit is the best way for them to determine that. Nearly every opportunity in life is affected by your credit. So in short, your credit is EXTREMELY important and impact everything!

Statistics

Some interesting statistics regarding credit reporting.

- 79% of credit reports surveyed by US PIRG contained errors or mistakes?
- Over 61 million Americans have subprime credit scores - Between 350-649.
- Nearly 33 million Americans do not have enough credit to generate a credit score.
- 24 million Americans have no credit file.

Most consumers have no idea how to get a copy of their credit reports! Incredible when you think about how much your credit impacts your life.

Big 3 Bureaus

Let's dive into the basics. There are 3 major credit bureaus and nearly a thousand smaller bureaus. Make no mistake, credit reporting is BIG business.

- **TransUnion** – is based in Chicago and provides service to approximately 45,000 businesses and approximately 500 million consumers worldwide. It is also the third-largest credit agency in the US.

- **Equifax** – was founded in 1899, and is the oldest of the three agencies. They gather and maintain information on over 400 million credit holders worldwide. Based in Atlanta, Georgia, Equifax is a global service provider with over 7,000 employees in 14 countries.

- **Experian** – is the largest of the 3, they are based in Ireland and employ over 17,000 employees. Their revenue last year was over 5 billion dollars!

Anatomy of a Credit Report

Even though there many different bureaus, all credit reports have the same basic structure and anatomy.

You will find your "**Personal Information**" – This includes your name, potential aliases, your Date of Birth, Social, Current Address, previous addresses and employment information.

Negative Accounts – are anything that wasn't paid or paid late. These are items you DO NOT want on your report because they lower your credit score.

Items you DO want are **Positive Accounts** – are any accounts that have been paid on time.

Public Records are typically court records such as judgments, liens, bankruptcies, child support and sometimes criminal histories.

Inquiries are a record of anytime your credit report has been requested. There are several types of inquiries and each have different meanings. I will be explaining this in greater detail in a few minutes.

Consumer Statements – to me, are ludicrous. I say that because it is essentially an area on your credit report that allows you to place a 100 words or less explanation about something on your credit. From my experience, adding a consumer statement never helps. If anything it can make you look guilty for something a lender wouldn't have even wondered about until you mention it.

Furnisher Contact Information includes the names, addresses and phone numbers of the companies that have reported information to the credit bureaus. This information is kept available to you, the consumer so you are able to contact anyone that has reported information about you.

Foreclosures – Foreclosures have recently skyrocketed after the collapse of the subprime mortgage industry. Foreclosures are extremely negative and usually high dollar amounts considering its real estate.

Duplicates - Duplicate entries, or instances where a particular situation shows up more than one time, on consumers credit reports can make it look as though they have more debt or credit issues than they really do, which can negatively affect chances of getting a loan or having credit extended. Some of the most common duplicate, triplicate or quadruplicate entries are medical bills, student loans, utility bills that have been sold to multiple collection agencies and/or any other item that gets sold and resold.

Other factors that impact credit scores negatively
Debt: The more debt you have, the higher credit risk lenders you are and the lower your score goes. Simple as that!

Not paying at all: Completely ignoring your bills is much worse than paying late. Each month you miss a credit card, auto loan, installment account or mortgage payment, you are one month closer to having the account charged off. Eventually, the creditor will consider the debt uncollectible and either sell or lease the debt to a 3rd party debt collector. We have seen thousands of instances where the original creditor continues to report the entire balance and an additional collection item appear in the collections section of consumer credit reports. This causes duplicates, triplicates and quadruplicates and excessive and incorrect balance amounts.

Having Accounts Sent a Collection Agency: Creditors often use third-party debt collectors to try to collect payment from you. Creditors might send your account to collections before or after charging it off. A collection status shows that the creditor gave up trying to get payment from you and hired someone else to do it.

Positive Items

Now that you know what can hurt your credit, let's discuss what will help it! "These Positive Items will increase your scores!"

Low Balances – are obviously better then high balances. Keep this important piece of information in mind throughout your life. EVERY DOLLAR OF DEBT YOU OWE IS CONSIDERED A RISK FACTOR - THE MORE DEBT YOU OWE, THE MORE LIKELY IT IS THAT YOU WILL NOT REPAY IT – AND….. EVERY DOLLAR OF DEBT WILL HURT YOUR CREDIT. This is a catch 22 for most people because you need to borrow money to build credit, but borrowing money hurts your credit at the same time. There is an old saying that goes: Banks are only interested in borrowing money to people that don't need it, and boy is that true!

On Time Payments are always going to be good. Doesn't matter if it's a credit card, home loan, auto loan, student loan or whatever… pay on time and it's "positive factor" that will only help you build your credit.

Aged Accounts – The older your open accounts are (with a positive credit history) the more likely it is that you will continue to pay on time; therefore – Old open accounts are positive and will improve your credit score.

You always want "**Accurate Information**" – Not only accurate account info, but just as important your personal information must be correct! There are a few reasons for this:

Your name for example: If you have multiple aliases or misspelled first, middle or last names – lenders may consider you a higher risk because it may be a sign that you are not who you say you are and possibly an identity thief. Or, how about your employment information..... If you are applying for credit, insurance or a job ... and your employment information is different then what is on your application, IT'S A RED FLAG. There are many other instances such as you address or social security number that need to be corrected.

Finally, let's talk about **diversifying your credit**. Lenders like to see that you are able to handle paying different types of account. This means "mixing it up". Having a "Mix" of Credit means that you have different types of accounts reporting to the credit bureaus. With that being said, if you only have installment loans, that could hinder your ability to get a home loan because your credit is not diversified. You would be much better off showing that you have experience paying installment and revolving accounts as well.

Calculating Credit Scores

So, what are credit scores and how are Credit Scores Calculated? Credit scores are basically adult financial GPA's! Seriously though, your score is your "financial reputation" and banks, lenders, employers, insurance companies and others take your reputation seriously.

There are many different types of credit scores. Thousands of companies sell their own whitelabeled credit reports and most use their own scoring models, so the score you get from one place to the next will typically be different. Regardless, the scores are intended to help you gauge how good or bad your credit is, but more importantly it's to help banks, lenders and other companies make complex, high-volume lending decisions.

Let's discuss how scores are calculated.

The biggest chunk of your credit score is primarily Payment History - (This is approximately 35% of your total score) - Late or missed payments obviously lower your credit score. In general risk scoring systems look for negative events like charge offs, collections, late payments, repossessions, foreclosures, settlements, bankruptcies, liens, and judgments. Within this category credit scores consider the severity of the negative item, the age of the negative items and the prevalence of negative items. Newer is worse than older. More severe is worse than less severe. And, many are worse than few. Basically, not paying on time can devastate your credit scores.

Debt is a huge factor and accounts for roughly 30% of your score. Scoring models consider the amount and type of debt carried as reflected on your credit reports. There are three types of debt considered.

- Revolving Debt
- Installment Debt
- Open Debt

Let's talk about each type of debt because it does matter...

1. Revolving Debt – This is usually a credit card, retail card, merchandise or gas cards Basically if you use it, then pay it and can use it again - it's considered revolving. The most important measurement from this category is called "Revolving Utilization" which is the relationship between the consumer's aggregate credit card balances and available credit card limits, also called "open to buy." This is expressed as a percentage and is calculated by dividing the aggregate credit card balances by the aggregate credit limits and multiplying the result by 100, thus yielding the utilization percentage. The higher that percentage the lower your score will likely be. This is why closing credit cards is generally not a good idea for someone trying to improve their credit scores. Closing one or more credit card accounts will reduce your total available credit limits and likely increase the utilization percentage unless the cardholder reduces their balances at the same pace.

2. Installment Debt – This is a debt where there is a fixed payment for a fixed period of time. An auto loan is a good example as you're generally making the same payment for 36, 48, or 60 months. While installment debt is considered in credit scores, it's not nearly as important as revolving and hold far less weight. Installment debt is generally secured by an asset like a car, home, or boat. Consumers will typically make a far greater effort on secured accounts to make their payments are on time, so their asset isn't repossessed by the lender for non-payment.

3. Open Debt – This is the least common type of debt. This is a debt that must be paid in full each month. A good example is a credit card that you are required to "pay in full" every month. The American Express platinum, Gold and Green cards are common examples.

- Your Credit History, also known as "Time on File" or "Credit File Age" accounts for 15% of your score. The reason why it impacts 15% of your scores is because lenders know that the older your credit is the more stable it is.

This "age" is determined two ways:

1. The age of your credit file and the average age of the accounts on your credit file. The age of your credit file is determined by the oldest account's "date opened", which sets the age of the credit file.

2. The average age is set by averaging the age of every account on the credit report, whether open or closed.

Account Diversity or also known as "Types of Credit Used" – This is approximately a 10% contribution to your credit score. Your credit score will benefit by having a diverse set of account types on your credit file. Having experience across multiple account types (installment, revolving, auto, mortgage, cards, etc.) is generally a good thing for your scores because you're proving the ability to manage different account types.

The Search for New Credit – (Also known as Credit inquiries) - Each time your credit is pulled by anyone except for you, it has an impact on your creditworthiness and your scores. A soft inquiry is when you pull your own credit and it does not impact your score, however when someone else pulls your credit – its considered a hard inquiry and is visible to lenders and credit scoring models. Keeping inquiries to a minimum can help your credit rating. A lender may perceive many inquiries over a short period of time on your report as a signal that you are having financial difficulty, and may consider you a higher risk. New credit and inquiries are about 10% of your score.

Quick Recap:

- 35% - Payment History: Negative information.
- 30% - Debt: How much and what type?
- 15% - Length Of Credit History: This is how long you've had credit

- 10% - Credit Diversity: This is the different types of credit experience you've had
- 10% - Inquiries (hard): This is when a creditor checks your credit report

Keep in mind, there are many other types of credit scores, each one uses its own scoring model.

How Debt Impacts Credit

Debt is the single most important factor on your credit! If there is any piece of information you should remember, it would be this: EVERY DOLLAR OF DEBT YOU OWE IS CONSIDERED A RISK FACTOR - THE MORE DEBT YOU OWE, THE MORE LIKELY IT IS THAT YOU WILL NOT REPAY IT – AND..... EVERY DOLLAR OF DEBT WILL HURT YOUR CREDIT.

Different types of debt have different impacts on your score.

Revolving account balances hurt more – this is because they can be reused. Again, credit is a numbers game and everything is mathematical and statistical. Credit scoring models use complex mathematical algorithms that determine the likelihood of repayment which in turn determines the risk assessment. Ideally, keep zero balances on your revolving credit accounts. Installment and secured accounts on the other hand hurt less – these may include homes, vehicles or personal loans. As long as they are not revolving like CREDIT CARDS, they will have a lesser impact on your credit and credit score.

Optimizing Credit Scores

Here are a few tips to optimize and increase credit scores. Of course, you only want positive and accurate information on your reports. If you do not, your credit will suffer. If you have mistakes, inaccuracies or outdated information on your credit report, there is a way to fix much of it. If you have negative information on your report, obviously you should begin repairing it, but there are also ways to minimize the items even if you are not successful removing them.

First, make sure you have a good mix of accounts. You should have at least one installment loan and three revolving credit cards. But, make sure you keep your revolving balances low! Pay down your revolving accounts such as credit cards first, try to keep them either very low or at zero balances.

Remember, you have to play to score! If you do not use your revolving credit cards every few months, they may stop reporting. Credit card companies PAY to report your account information to the credit agencies. Accounts that are idle or show no activity will stop being reported. I recommend that you buy a small ticket item with each card about every 90 days to keep them reporting. So you can use your accounts BUT keep your balances as low as possible.

If you have been paying on time, most creditors are happy to increase your credit lines. Some of them do it automatically, some do not. Try calling each credit card company every 6 months or so and tell them that you would like them to increase your credit line.

Your oldest accounts are your most valuable when it comes to your credit scores. It's important to keep them open. Even if there is a yearly or monthly fee, consider keeping them open because closing an old credit card could damage your score!

Another important tip is opening and maintaining new accounts that report to the credit bureaus is key to building a solid credit rating. There are many different types of accounts that you can be approved for even with a poor credit rating. Typically, you will pay a higher interest rate, higher fees or may have to secure the account with collateral such as money or assets in order to open accounts if your credit is less than perfect. Credit history accounts for about 35% of credit scores; therefore if you don't have sufficient credit history you need to open new accounts and pay the price if you ever want to increase your score.

We covered a little bit about inquiries earlier and how they impact your credit. Each time you apply for credit, an inquiry will appear and can drag your credit score down a few points, so try not to apply for credit unless you are either trying to build credit or absolutely need something!

Lastly, make sure your personal information is accurate and up to date. This includes your name, address, previous addresses, social, date of birth and employment history. When lenders or potential employers pull your credit, they may check to make sure the information you placed on your application matches what the credit bureaus have on file. If not, they may consider you a risk because of it.

Piggybacking

There is a technique that does work and not many people know about it and many of those that do, don't really understand enough to make it work. I'm going to explain it in detail for you.

One of the fastest and easiest ways to add instant credit history is by piggybacking.

There are two different ways you can "Piggyback"

1. Authorized User
2. Joint Account Holder

Each has its advantages and disadvantages and I'll explain what those are.

What is piggybacking and which method should I choose?

Piggybacking is a technique that allows you to inherit someone else's credit history by being added to an account - typically a credit card.

It can season your credit and increase your credit scores.

When the general public caught on to this trick a few years ago, it spawned an entire industry to meet consumer demand. There are companies that you can pay to piggyback a complete strangers credit card account.

They call these companies "tradeline dealers" who pay cardholders to rent out spots on their cards, but only as authorized users. Some credit card companies allow 20 or more authorized users, so these tradeline dealers charge anywhere from a few hundred to thousands of dollars to rent these spots. The authorized user never gets an actual credit card, but the account will typically show up on their report. Looks great!

Eventually the banks, lenders and credit scoring providers caught on and the scoring models shifted the weight of authorized users to minimize this practice. With that being said, authorized users on most cards do not carry much weight and have a much lesser impact unless the primary on the account is a family member or spouse of the authorized user.

*IMPORTANT: There are many companies that sell tradelines - STAY AWAY from them! Any person buying tradelines in an attempt to cheat or defraud a mortgage score may result in mortgage fraud which is a felony and could result in jail time! Do not buy, sell or partner with any tradeline dealer or broker. On the other hand, if you ask a family member to help you - that is completely legal.

Here is how Piggybacking works:

1st Find someone you trust. This person must have a credit card account with a major bank in good standing with a low or preferably no balance. Also you want to choose an aged account - one that has a long history - the older the better. And finally the primary must be willing to add you to the account.

- I say in good standing because you don't want to inherit a negative account, right?
- I said "preferably low or no balance" because if the account has high balance or is maxed out, it will only hurt your scores.
- Lastly, I mentioned you want an aged account - why? The older the account is, the longer the payment history is and that will help your credit the most.

2nd Now your friend or family member calls the credit card company and requests to add you as an authorized user or joint account holder.

- The credit card companies are usually more than happy to add someone else to the account.

- So, should you choose "authorized user" or "joint account holder"? That depends on a few things. Just try to remember this:
  1. Credit scoring models will not place much weight on authorized users unless the primary is your spouse or family member.

  2. As an authorized user, you have zero liability. If the account ever falls behind, has late payments or the primary maxes the card out, you can have it removed from your credit just as easy as it was to add it. Just call the creditor and ask them, they will remove you and remove it from your credit.

  3. Now, on the other hand - if you choose to be a joint account holder, you are permanently responsible for that credit card forever! It's really important that you make sure that the primary account holder is a responsible person and intends on paying on time and keeping the balance low otherwise there is a good possibility that you will end up with problems. If the primary maxes out the account, is late, goes to collections, gets a judgment or files bankruptcy - you are equally responsible for it, just as if you cosigned. Unlike an authorized user, you cannot simply ask to be removed - it's permanent. So be VERY careful.

3rd Be sure you monitor your credit reports to make sure it gets reported to the credit reporting agencies. Provided you did everything correctly; this account should show up on your credit reports within 30-60 days.

- The next time a lender pulls your credit report it will recalculate all (3) credit scores and include the account as if it was yours.

- The entire payment history will appear on your credit report and will be calculated into their new scores.

- I've seen this technique work wonders to boost scores, but I have also seen it cause catastrophic problems not only with credit scores, but relationships with friends and family. My best advice would be to do your due diligence and be careful who you share accounts with.

Lesson #2 **Common Credit Issues**

Now that we have a basic understanding of credit, let's talk a little bit about what to look for when analyzing a credit report. We're talking about all the most common issues you may find on your credit.

It doesn't matter if it's your personal credit report or if it's for a friend, family member or for a client, everyone has the right to dispute anything that is questionable.

When I say "questionable - that includes:

- Any item you do not feel it's 100% factually correct.

Inaccurate could mean...

- Errors, Mistakes and Duplicate Accounts
- Excessive Inquiries
- Conflicting personal information, like a misspelled name, the wrong date of birth..
- Mixed Credit Files (where your father with the same name is mixed with yours, or maybe even a stranger with the same name is mixed up on your credit file...)
- Or of course there may be Identity theft or Fraud or where someone opened an account using your identity.

- These are all questionable!

You also have the right to remove anything which is outdated. When I say outdated, I'm talking about the length of time the account or negative item has been on your report. There are different rules for how long negative information can appear based on several factors. I'll teach you all those rules in the next lesson, for now let's learn how to analyze and find all the problems!

How to Find the Errors

Let's talk about how to find the errors on a credit report. It's pretty easy to spot them when you know what to look for. If you have a copy of a credit report, now would be a great time to print it out and follow along as I go through all the different sections of the report.

Depending on the source of the credit report, the format may look different, but all credit reports have the same general 4 sections:

- Identifying Information
- Public Records
- Credit History
- Inquiries

Personal Information

Let's take a look at the "Identifying Information" section, also known as "Personal Information".

This area will list your name, social, current and previous address, telephone number, date of birth, current and previous employers and sometimes your spouse's name.

Where do the credit bureaus get this information? Well, whenever you apply for credit, or an employer pulls your credit, or anyone else for that matter - they must input identifying information about you and that information becomes part of your credit file. Human error is one of the main reasons why this information may be wrong.

Accurate personal information is important for a few reasons.

1. You don't want to be confused with someone else, their bad credit may show up on your report as a mixed credit file.
2. Lenders check it and if your personal information doesn't match up with what you wrote on your application, it can be a red flag and grounds for denial.
3. Employers may pull your credit, even insurance companies often check your credit.

Here are some things you can look for in the personal information section:

- Look for any incorrect or incomplete name listed. If you see your name is misspelled - circle it!
- Check your current address - then check to make sure your prior addresses are correct and complete. If not, circle them!
- Make sure your Social Security number and date of birth is accurate.
- Your employment information is important because employers will often check it to make sure your resume is not misleading... Look for incorrect, missing, or outdated employment information.
- Believe it or not, but sometimes you could be mistakenly identified as "deceased". This happens if a creditor reports an account as associated with a deceased individual or if your Social Security Number was

reported as deceased. If you are accidentally listed as deceased, you won't be able to get a bank account, renew your driver's license, get health insurance, find an apartment, or participate in many other every day activities.

Public Records

Next, look at the Public Records section of your report. This section should include any court filings like bankruptcies, judgments, liens, lawsuits and foreclosures and have a serious impact on your report. Just like any other item on your credit report, there may be errors.

This is what you should be looking for:

- Do you see any lawsuits appearing that you were not involved in?
- You may see a bankruptcy filed by a spouse or ex-spouse, even though you did not file bankruptcy.
- If you filed bankruptcy over 10 years ago, they shouldn't be there.
- Sometimes you may see a bankruptcy which is not identified by the specific chapter of the bankruptcy code, that is grounds for removal.
- Look for lawsuits or judgments older than seven years after the judgment was entered, or after the statute of limitations expired. (I'll go more in depth about how long items can stay on your report in the next lesson.)
- For example tax liens you paid more than seven years ago, or criminal arrest records more than seven years old shouldnt be appearing.

There are rules for how long information can stay on your report - don't worry I'll go over all of this and I'll even give you some cheat sheets to print out - so make sure you have downloaded all the documents attached to lesson 1.

Lesson #3 Using Laws to Repair Credit

The fundamental idea of credit repair revolves around your rights as a consumer. The rights you have are all based around a handful of Federal and state laws.

So what is credit repair?

Basic credit repair is a legal way to delete inaccurate, incomplete and outdated negative credit history by disputing items on your credit.

This can be done by disputing items with the credit bureaus OR with furnishers that reported the information, like creditors and debt collectors.

With the Fair Credit Reporting Act and other laws, you have the legal right to dispute any information on your report. Then, the credit bureaus and furnishers have 30 days to investigate and either verify it as correct or remove the disputed information.

They are also required to mail you the results within 30 days.

So when you get the results, you will know what happened and decide on what to do next.

We call these monthly cycles or batches of letters "Rounds"... So the first batch of letters is called round 1, then round 2,, round 3 etc.

We'll dive deeper into this process later on, for now; this lesson will give you a basic understanding of the laws and how to use them to your advantage.

Fair Credit Reporting Act (FCRA)

There are a bunch of different laws - but, the most useful piece of legislation for credit repair is called the Federal Fair Credit Reporting Act. This set of laws was enacted to promote the accuracy, fairness, and privacy of your personal information related to your credit. It's the primary set of laws that makes credit repair possible.

These laws have REALLY long names, so we like to use acronyms to shorten them up. We're going to call this set of laws the "F.C.R.A." for now on!

Reminder, this is a beginner course, so without going into too much detail, some of the rights you have under the FCRA:

1. You have the right to know what's in your credit file.

2. You must be notified if the information in your credit file has been used against you.

3. You have the right to dispute incomplete or inaccurate information and the credit bureau must correct or delete it within 30 days from the time they receive your dispute.

4. Credit bureaus may not report outdated information. (I will discuss this in greater detail)

5. Your file may only be shared with people or companies with a valid need, usually to consider an application for credit, employment, insurance or renting.

6. So, you know all that junk mail you get from companies stating your pre approved? They get your information from the credit bureaus, they are called prescreened credit offers - and you have the right to block those companies from buying that information.

7. Another right you have as a consumer under the FCRA is to block your report if you feel you may be a victim of identity theft. You have the right to place a security freeze to stop the bureaus from releasing your personal information. You can also remove the freeze when you see fit.

8. If your rights were violated, you may seek damages.

By the way, when I say: "You may seek damages", the FCRA is very specific. Each occurrence can leave the bureau or furnisher financially liable and you don't need to sue them yourself - most credit repair companies work with local attorneys that will sue them for you on a contingency basis, meaning you don't pay unless they collect.

So that was a summary of the Fair Credit Reporting Act, seems pretty simple right? The FCRA is powerful when used properly.

Again, I have included a downloadable PDF copy of the FCRA on lesson 1.

Fair Debt Collection Practices Act (FDCPA)

Ok, so here's another long name for ya! The Federal Fair Debt Collection Practices Act is the legislation that governs the debt collection industry. For the sake of simplicity, let's call it the FDCPA for short.

These laws were enacted specifically to provide limitations on what debt collectors can do when collecting on certain types of debt. The FDCPA prohibits debt collection companies from using abusive, unfair or deceptive practices to collect debts from you.

Debt collectors include collection agencies, debt buyers and lawyers who regularly collect debts as part of their business. There are also companies that buy past due accounts from creditors or other businesses and then try to collect them. These debt collectors are also usually called debt collection agencies, debt collection companies, or debt buyers.

The FDCPA restricts debt collectors from calling you before or after certain hours and also does not allow any form of harassment. Additionally, if you have an attorney representing you, the debt collector must contact your attorney instead of you after it is known.

Most importantly, as it relates to credit repair - the FDCPA can help you place the burden of proof on the debt collector if you dispute the validity of the debt.

Also, debt collectors must send consumers a letter with some basic information on the debt within five days of first contacting them. It must include the amount of debt, original creditors name and a summary of your rights.

If you dispute a debt in writing or demand validation within 30 days of when you receive the required information from the debt collector, the debt collector cannot call or contact you to collect the debt or the disputed part until the debt collector has provided verification of the debt in writing to you. This is often very helpful in removing accounts from your credit report that cannot be verified.

I once helped a client that had a debt collector trying to collect a really large debt, it was over 60k. The debt collector was calling him at work, late at night and really causing a lot of problems. When I became aware of the issue, I mailed a simple validation demand to the debt collector. I asked for the written contract for the account they were trying to collect and they were not able to produce it. Then I disputed the account with the credit bureaus and viola! It was deleted and the debt collector crawled back under the rock he came from.

So, as you can see the Fair Debt Collection Practices Act is quite powerful, once you know how to use it!

Here is a quick recap:

1. The Fair Debt Collection Practices Act is called the FDCPA for short.
2. The FDCPA covers when, how, and how often a third-party debt collector can contact a debtor.
3. The FDCPA makes it illegal for debt collectors to use abusive, unfair, or deceptive practices when they collect debts. Basically no harassment or unfair treatment.
4. If the FDCPA is violated, you can sue the debt collector in a state or federal court for damages plus legal fees, some attorneys do it on a contingency basis.

This lesson is a basic introduction, I highly recommend that you read the full document and learn more with our advanced lessons. I've included a downloadable copy of it for you to read and keep! You should keep them handy while I go through this lesson!

Statute of Limitations

A "Statute of Limitations" is = Length of time an action is valid.

There are statutes of limitations on all sorts of things. Today we're talking about credit and debt so in regards to today's lesson the Statute of Limitations is a definitive amount of time items can appear on your credit and how long debts can be collected.

There are two primary statutes of limitations: "Debt Collection" and "Credit Reporting".

Attachments

For the sake of simplicity, we're going to call them the "Credit Time Clock" and the "Debt Time Clock."

Again, the credit time clock is maximum amount of time items can appear on your credit report. And, the Debt Time Clock is the maximum amount of time someone can bring legal action on a debt you owe.

I created 2 awesome charts that you can download and keep. Please make sure you do that, they will come in handy. You can find them in this section of your course software.

We are going to start with "Credit Timeclock."

Credit Time Clock

So, the "Credit Time Clock" is essentially the Statute of Limitations for Credit Reporting...

There's a bunch of names for it - Officially called "running of reporting period", is also called the statute of limitations for credit reporting and some people call it the 7 year rule - I call it the Credit Time Clock and it's one of the most misunderstood parts of the fair credit reporting act.

The Fair Credit Reporting Act describes how long items can remain on credit reports and when they must be removed. Some items have a seven year expiration date like charge-offs and collections while other items remain for 10 years like bankruptcies - in the case of tax liens, they may remain indefinitely.

The credit bureaus keep personal credit history for a specific amount of time based on the items DATE of FIRST DELINQUENCY.

The DATE of FIRST DELINQUENCY is when you stopped paying.

The following information is taken directly from the Fair Credit Reporting Act (FCRA) and from the Federal Trade Commission's official interpretation of the "running of reporting period!"

- Derogatory Accounts can stay for - 7 years from the DATE of FIRST DELINQUENCY!
- Inquiries – they can stay for 2 years from the date placed, some soft inquiries only stay for 6 months!
- Unpaid Tax Liens can stay "Indefinitely"
- Chapter 7 Bankruptcy is 10 years from the date filed.
- Chapter 13 Bankruptcy (also called a repayment plan) can stay for 7 years from the date the repayment plan ends.... This means that if you have a 4 year repayment plan, it could take as long as 11 years to "fall off" your credit report.
- The majority of Public Records like judgments and child support take 7 years.
- Closed or Inactive Accounts generally fall off after 10 years.

One important thing I'd like to mention is that you would expect items to automatically "fall off" your credit report when the time clock is over. This unfortunately isn't always the case!

Sometimes, errors are made and OFTEN creditors or debt collectors will purposely report false "status" dates in hopes of keeping items on your credit report longer.

The reason they do this is because the longer something negative is on your report, the more likely it is that you eventually pay it. This is illegal, but more common than you would think.

Debt Time Clock

The Debt Time Clock also called the "Debt Collection Statute of Limitations" This is the length of time a debt collection agency can take a legal action to collect a debt.

The length of time to bring action is determined by the type of contract (Written, Oral, Promissory or Open Ended Accounts) and is also determined by the STATE in which the debtor lived in when the debt began in.

Let's discuss the "Types of Debt" and then I'll give some examples regarding the varying states.

1. **Oral Contract:** You agree to pay money loaned to you by someone, but this contract or agreement is verbal (i.e., no written contract, "handshake agreement"). Remember a verbal contract is legal, but tougher to prove in court.

2. **Written Contract:** You agree to pay on a loan under the terms written in a document, which you and your debtor have signed.

3. **Promissory Note:** You agree to pay on a loan via a written contract, just like the written contract. The big difference between a promissory note and a regular written contract is that the scheduled payments and interest on the loan also is spelled out in the promissory note. A mortgage is an example of a promissory note.

4. **Open-ended Accounts:** These are revolving lines of credit with varying balances. The best example is a credit card account.

Ok, now - let's chat about expired debt!

Expired Debt

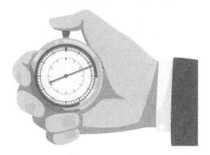

I'd like to talk a little more about the debt time clock in relation to when the debt actually expires.

Its determined by two factors:

1. The type of debt and..
2. The state the debtor lives in.
   - I have attached a copy of the state by state chart that outlines the statute of limitations for collection of debt that is pretty easy to understand. Please print it out and have it handy so you can follow along.
   - I've personally used this chart hundreds if not thousands of times to help my clients.
   - Knowing if a debt is expired or not gives you an edge.

The chart you see on my screen is a screenshot of the chart I attached to this lesson.

Once you understand it, it's pretty awesome to be able to answer questions for any situation.

For Example:
Let's say you stopped paying a credit card debt in the state of Florida and it was sold to ABC collections, and ABC collections is coming after you. They're calling you, sending letters and threatening to sue. They want the money and they want it now! The statute of limitations protects you. In this example, if it

is a "credit card", that would mean it's "open ended". We went over this a few minutes ago - revolving accounts that you can use, pay back - then reuse... means "open ended". You would simply scroll down to Florida, then go to the "Open-Ended" column. It says 4 years. So, with that being said, the length of time the creditor has to collect the debt is 4 years from the date of last activity. The "Date of Last Activity" is when you last made a payment. If you never made any payments, it would be the date you opened the account. So, in this example, if your last payment was over 4 years ago, technically, you no longer owe this debt. it's no longer valid.

Let's do another example:

Let's say you live in Louisiana, you had a personal loan and you stopped paying it. That would be considered a written contract. Once you've signed the written contract, you're bound by the terms of the contract. If you default on the terms of the contract by failing to make the payments as agreed, the other party may take certain actions to pursue you for what you owe. One of those actions could include filing a lawsuit against you to get you to pay up.

If they decide to sue you, they would have 10 years before the debt would be expired. Ok.

I would also like to point out that they would be able to sue you after the 10 year expiration date - but if you can prove that the debt is expired it's highly unlikely they would win.

Knowing when debts expire is helpful for many reasons.

1. Creditors and debt collectors know that most consumers don't understand how long debts are valid, and being able to stand up for your rights or help clients do the same is very powerful.
2. Knowing when debt expire gives you a big advantage if you are ever sued.
3. It gives you leverage.

I would highly recommend you print and keep copies of the charts I attached to this lesson, they will come in handy.

Lesson #4 **Basic Credit Repair Strategies**

Now that you have a basic understanding of the laws to use, let's talk about how to use them! This lesson will cover all the basics of how to write dispute letters. We will cover some of the basic dispute strategies and most importantly, I'll give you a solid understanding of my top 10 favorite letters and when to use them.

Bureau Disputes

Let's talk about the basic strategies for repairing credit.

The first strategy is generally the easiest, sending letters directly to the credit bureaus for a few reasons:

1. You can dispute as many items as you like, but I highly recommend you don't overdo it. You will usually get a better response by only disputing up to 5 items maximum.

2. The credit bureaus are required to contact the furnishers that reported the information for you, so you do not need to contact the furnishers individually - it's all done for you.

3. After the bureaus contact the furnishers, they only have 30 days to respond. If they don't respond in time, the items you disputed automatically get deleted.

In the next lesson, I will explain all of this in much greater detail. For now, just know that contacting the credit bureaus should be your first line of attack.

Furnisher Disputes

The next strategy is disputing directly with your furnishers, again "furnisher" means the companies (creditors and debt collection agencies) that reported the information to the credit bureaus in the first place. You have the right to dispute with these companies and they are required to investigate and report any changes to the credit bureaus.

This can be a long drawn out process for a few reasons:

1. Typically you can only dispute one item at a time unless you have more than one account with the same creditor.

2. Creditors and collection agencies are notorious for completely ignoring disputes and holding them accountable is generally more difficult with furnishers, especially some of the smaller rogue agencies.

I'll get into the nuts and bolts of furnisher disputes in the next lesson.

Other Strategies

Disputing with the bureaus and furnishers are the two most common and simple strategies when repairing credit.

This is a basic disputing course, so I'm not going into details about the other strategies at this time but I'd like to at least give you an idea of what else is possible to help you gain an understanding of other strategies that also work wonders.

1. Creditor Interventions are also sometimes called a "goodwill intervention". The letter works by sending it to the creditor asking them very nicely to remove a late payment. This normally works best on OPEN accounts that you have an excellent payment history and simply missed one payment. Even though they are not required to do so, many companies will respond positively and remove the late payment.

2. If you have completely exhausted your efforts in disputing a collection account, and you have little hope it will be removed, you always have the option of attempting to settle the stubborn debt. To do this, you need to strike a deal with the creditor by negotiating. Usually this is done over the phone or by mail, either way you want to make sure you have an agreement in writing before paying.

3. Once you have exhausted your efforts with both the credit bureaus and furnishers, and mistakes are still appearing on your credit report, you may want to consider filing a lawsuit. If the errors are not corrected, it may be time to get the help of a consumer protection lawyer. The Fair Credit Reporting Act (FCRA) and other laws we spoke about were put in place to help protect you. There are many consumer protection attorneys that will go to work for you on a contingency basis. You don't pay them unless they win and when they do, you get paid and get the errors removed permanently.

One often overlooked strategy to credit repair is to build positive credit, which in turn reduces the impact of any negative credit on your reports. In lesson one, I went over a ton of ways to build and optimize your credit scores.

Put all of that into action so you can improve your credit from every angle possible.

The Anatomy of a Basic Dispute Letter

Credit repair is all about sending letters. I'd like for you to really understand how dispute letters are built and what to include.

The good news is, Credit Repair Cloud has an entire library of the most effective dispute letters that have been time tested and used literally millions of times over. Still, I'd like you to have a deeper understanding in case you want to do it on your own without software.

There are several things you want to insure are included in every dispute letter you send.

1. **The Heading:** Include Identifying Information - Make sure your letter contains the accurate spelling of your first, middle and last name. You should also include your current home address and the last 4 your social security number. No need to include your full social, only the last 4 digits are necessary.

2. **The Inside Address Include:** the Recipient's Identifying Information - Depending on who your sending it to, include the recipient name and address. This is usually one of the 3 credit bureaus or a creditor or debt collector.

3. **Always include a Subject Line:** This is a quick blurb that summarizes the contents of the letter. For example: "Validation requested for account that does not belong to me."

4. **The body of the letter** is the longest part of a letter and is usually divided into three subcategories: introduction, main content and summary. The introductory paragraph states the purpose of the letter. The main content conveys all necessary detailed information and has no set length requirements. The last paragraph summarizes the

information provided, restates the letter intent and offers instructions regarding follow-up correspondence.

5. **Furnisher Name(s) & Account Number(s):** Online credit reports will never show the full account number, so just add whatever is listed on the credit report, even if it's mostly X's and a few numbers. I'd like to point out that if you are mailing this letter to a credit bureau, the credit bureau will contact the furnisher to conduct the investigation - so getting this information is critical to the success of the letter.

6. **The Reason:** Each item you dispute needs a REASON to remove each item. Credit Repair Cloud software makes this remarkably easy. You simply choose the reason from a dropdown list.

   Some of the most common reasons:

   - The following information is not mine.
   - The information is inaccurate, please remove it!
   - The following information is outdated and I want it removed from my report.

   It's usually a sentence or two explaining why you want it changed. Pretty easy right?

7. **Next - The Instructions:** This is where you need to explain what you want to happen. You need to place a sentence or two to clearly describe the outcome you want as an instruction to the recipient.

   Some Common Instructions Include :

   1. Please correct or update the information on my credit report.
   2. Please remove this misleading information from my credit.
   3. Please investigate and remove this inaccurate information.

8. **Don't forget to sign the letter! Credit Repair Cloud software will automatically insert your clients signature into the letter digitally.**

9. **Also, always Include Identification for Round 1 Credit Bureau Disputes:** The credit bureaus require you to supply supporting documentation verifying your identity and your address. This is done by including a government issued photo ID (like a driver's license or passport) plus proof of address (like a utility bill, insurance statements, bank statement, etc)

Again, once your establish identity and address verification, you do not need to send the identification with the following letters, only Round 1, and only when disputing with the credit bureaus. That's it!

Now don't forget, we are going to be using my top 10 favorite letters that we previously discussed during this important lesson. You should have them printed out by now to help you follow along!

Top 10 Most Effective Dispute Letters

I'm going to introduce you to my top 10 favorite dispute letters.

Credit Repair Cloud has over 100 letters for every possible situation, however; this is a "Beginners Course" so I have chosen 10 of my favorite and most effective dispute letters and have outlined how to use them. If you learn how to use these 10 simple letters effectively, you will discover the fundamental building blocks of credit repair and be on your way to becoming an expert.

#1 Default Round 1 (Dispute Credit Report Items)

This should always be the first letter you send, and it should always be sent to the credit bureaus. Why? As previously discussed, you can dispute as many items as you like, the bureaus will contact each furnisher for you and if they don't respond within 30 days, it's an automatic deletion.

#2 Bureau No Response

The title of this letter also gives away it's meaning - when you send a letter to a credit bureau and they do not respond, this is the letter to send! Why? The credit bureaus are required under federal law to conduct an investigation and respond with the results of the investigation within 30 day of receiving your request. Ignoring the request is unacceptable and unfortunately, you may need to remind them more than once to comply.

#3 Bureau Re-investigation

So you've already disputed items with a credit bureau at least once or twice and didnt get the response you wanted. The reinvestigation letter is a good way to let the credit bureau know you are not giving up! It's amazing to me how much a little bit of patience and persistence can yield results and this letter is exactly that - persistent! So, when they say no - what do you do? You ask again and again and again. The squeaky wheel gets the grease!

#4 Bureau Warning

When you contact a credit bureau and either receive a bad response, or no response at all - it may be time to fire a warning shot. The credit bureaus will all too often play games by responding inappropriately. They may accuse you of utilizing a credit repair company - which by the way is entirely up to you and 100% legal. In some cases they may simply deem your request frivolous or ignore it all together. When this happens, you must remain persistent and not take it personally; however, you should absolutely fight back. One of the best ways to do this is with a well crafted warning letter. In the letter, you remind the credit bureau of your rights as a consumer, state the facts, include previous correspondence and/or any proof you may have - and most importantly, make it crystal clear that you mean business.

All the letters I discussed so far were all geared towards the credit bureaus. Those 4 letters are really all you need for "basic" credit repair with the bureaus.

Let's switch gears, the rest of my Top 10 letters are specifically for sending to furnishers. Again, furnishers are the companies that reported the information to the credit bureaus. They are typically creditors or debt collectors.

#5 Furnisher Basic Dispute

The furnisher dispute letter is virtually the same letter as the credit bureau dispute letter, the only difference is a slight change in the wording. You are using federal law to demand either deletion or correction to information that the creditor or debt collector reported about you to the credit bureau.

#6 Furnisher No Response

The furnisher no response letter template is virtually identical to the one you send the credit bureau, only with some slight wordsmithing. You are following up on a previous letter that was ignored.

#7 Furnisher Re-investigation

The Furnisher Reinvestigation Letter is also very much like the credit bureau reinvestigation letter. The name gives it away! Your asking the furnisher for another investigation!

#8 Furnisher Warning

The furnisher warning letter is very very similar to the credit bureau warning. There are slight changes to the content that make it more suitable to send to a furnisher. When they ignore you or don't comply with the laws, this letter is sending a clear warning that you are not taking no for an answer.

#9 Validation

If you're facing an aggressive debt collector - this debt validation letter can pause collection efforts and may deter debt collectors who don't have sufficient information.

If the debt is expired, you can include a sentence or two explaining that and it may not only stop collection activity but could possibly get it deleted from your credit report.

Also, if you intend on paying the debt, you might want more information to verify you're paying the right collector for the right debt.

If the debt is nearing its statute of limitations, you may be better off ignoring debt collection notices than drawing more attention to yourself with a validation letter so don't forget to check the chart I gave you in the previous lesson.

#10 Estoppel By Silence

The estoppel letter is used when a debt collector ignores your request for validation (This is the last letter we just discussed) So, basically if you give the debt collector the opportunity to speak up and validation the debt, they fail to do so and their silence must mean that they agree with you. So, it's always good to send this Estoppel Letter certified mail and include your previous validation demand letter. It can stop a debt collector dead in their tracks and sometimes result in a deletion from your credit report!

There you have it, those are my favorites for basic dispute strategies. In the final lessons, I will show you how to use them!

Lesson #5 **Sending Your 1st Dispute Letters**

In the previous lessons, I gave you the basics about credit and went over how to spot questionable information and mistakes. You also now have knowledge about the laws and how to use them to your advantage. It's time to use it! Are you ready?

This lesson will give you a clear understanding on how to get started sending your first letters and help guide you along the basic dispute process. I'm going to help you visualize the process of credit repair, and how to get started. If you have not already done so, please print out the attachment labeled "Basic Dispute Process" to follow along.

Grab the Low Hanging Fruit
(What to dispute first)

When I say grab the low hanging fruit, what I mean by that is - you want to remove as much negative information as possible with the least amount of effort. This is done in one of two ways:

1. Verification
2. Factual Disputing

Let's make sure we all understand the terminology.

> **Verification** is when you place the burden of proof on the credit bureaus to "VERIFY" questionable information.

> **Factual Disputing** is when you are disputing the item based on the fact that something about the item is inaccurate, outdated or incomplete.

A lot of people get both of these terms confused with Validation. Just to clear the air and hopefully provide some clarity - Validation is when you are demanding a 3rd party debt collection agency or furnisher to provide proof the account is accurate, this is not sent to the bureaus, it's sent directly to the debt collector.

So, when your're sending off your first dispute letters, I always recommend you start with the path of least resistance which is verification.

You can choose Round 1 as your letter, and the only thing you need to change are two things:

1. the REASON to suggest that you feel the items are questionable and...

2. the INSTRUCTION to state that you want the bureau to verify the items are 100% accurate or remove them. You'll be surprised at how many items are deleted simply because the furnisher fails to respond to the bureaus in 30 days.

So go ahead and request verification of a few items at a time.

If you are aware of any actual errors, or inaccurate, outdated or incomplete information, you can also start "factually Disputing" if you like.

For example, if you settled a collection account and have a written agreement that the account would be deleted - go ahead and include that proof and factually dispute it as one of your first items.

Then, maybe you have a late payment showing up that is over 7 years old, dispute that as well.

The idea of factual disputing is to try to pinpoint errors and inaccuracies if at all possible as opposed to just sending a bunch of blanket disputes.

Start with the 3 Bureaus Using Round 1

I want to let you in on a dirty little secret, most of the largest credit repair companies in America, the ones making millions and millions of dollars selling credit repair, use the same Round 1 letter in 90% of the letters they send. It may seem basic, but it is highly effective. After you have decided what to dispute, it's time to put it in writing.

Credit Repair Cloud's awesome software makes this process incredibly easy. It can automatically import your credit reports and pre-populate everything, so you simply choose the letter you want, then choose the reasons and instructions from a dropdown menu and click print.

You can also do this on your own without software, but you're going to need to know a little more about the process.

Your looking at an infographic flowchart. This is the first step in that chart. If you haven't already done so - please download the attached document labeled "Basic Dispute Process". This chart will help you fully understand what letters to send, when to send them and why.

There are some basic rules you should know if you want the letter to be effective:

1. Always use "Round 1 Letter" first! (it's simple for a reason) You can find the Round 1 letter attached to this lesson! (See in the illustration, this is the first step in the process.)

2. You should not dispute more than 5 items with each credit bureau. Here's why I recommend this: If you dispute too many items all at once, the credit bureau may deem your disputes as "frivolous," essentially throwing them all out -- and then you're fighting that as well. So if you're just starting out, keeping it under 5 items will give you a much easier start.

3. Remember, there are 3 credit bureaus (Experian, Equifax and TransUnion), each maintains their own separate records so, for example Experian may have items that Transunion does not have, or Equifax may not have items appearing on Experian. Make sure you review all 3 reports!

Reasons and Instructions

Make sure you include a REASON and INSTRUCTION for each item you are disputing! A lot of people are intimidated by this because they often feel the credit bureaus will read the instructions and disagree, but the truth of it is that there is very little human intervention.

*Note: When creating letters in Credit Repair Cloud, you will see the most common reasons and instructions already listed, and you can just click to choose the most appropriate one.

The credit bureaus automate 95% of their dispute handling. From the time the letter is actually received, there are machines that do almost everything. From slicing upon the envelope to scanning an image of the letter, a computer does almost everything - it even reads the letter.

Depending on which bureau it is, the only decision making humans have in the process is determining the reason and instruction for each item. They don't care about the content of the letter, they just want to know what is being disputed and why it's being disputed so they can place a numerical value on the item and feed it back into their computer system which automatically, electronically contacts the furnisher that reported it.

Regardless, I can tell you from vast experience in writing dispute letters - although the reason and instruction for each item is required - it's not all that important. Frankly, what you are counting on is for the furnisher to not respond - so the account is deleted. As long as that happens - mission accomplished.

Let's discuss some common "reasons":

1. If the item doesn't belong to you, you can simply list the furnisher name and account number, followed by the reason. The reason can be very simple like: "The following information is not mine."

2. Or, another example.. If you feel the information is wrong, or questionable, there is no need to go into details, you can say something like: "The information is inaccurate, please remove it!"

3. Or, let's say that one of the items is past the credit reporting time clock, you can say something simple as "The following information is outdated and I want it removed from my report." OR, you can get specific and say "The status date for this collection account is over 7 years old and should not appear on my report.

It's really up to you. There is no real "wrong way" to explain what you want done, just make sure you include a reason with each item your disputing.

Alright, so we talked about the reasons to remove, each item should also have an instruction. This is super easy. You are basically telling the credit bureau what to do for each item. Always try to be polite as possible and state what you want to happen.

For example, let's say you have a late payment on an open account. You don't want the entire account deleted, you just want to late payment removed. You can say something like this: "Please correct my report by removing the late payment from my credit report."

Or, this time - let's do an example where you have a collection account that doesn't belong to you. You can say: "Please remove this misleading information from my credit." I think you get the idea by now, it's very simple to explain what result you want.

Let's do one final example:

Let's say the collection account your disputing is yours, but it has the wrong status date, the wrong balance or something about it is questionable. Every item on your report must be 100% accurate or removed. I would say something like "Please investigate and remove this inaccurate information."

Ok great, you've got this!

Include Photo ID and Proof of Address

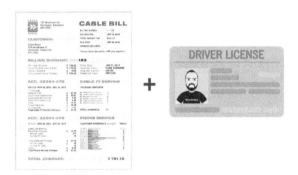

Ok so at this point, you've reviewed your credit reports, decided on what items you want to dispute first, your using round 1 dispute letter and you are either using Credit Repair Cloud Software to make it easy, or you are manually writing your own letters for each of the 3 bureaus.

You have listed up to 5 items you want to dispute on each of the 3 letters, and have added the names, account numbers, reasons and instructions for each item your disputing..

Your letters look great, what do you do next?

When you're ready to mail out your first round letters to the bureaus, make sure you include ID and address verification documents, the credit bureaus will not send you the results unless you prove you are who you say you are and prove where you live. The best verification documents are a government issued ID plus a utility bill with your current address.

Once you verify your identity, you do not need to send the verification documents for later rounds. Some people send the documents with every dispute just to be sure the process doesn't slow down or stop, but that is entirely up to you.

If you have proof, include it!

Remember a few minutes ago, I said that if you have proof - you should use it. Let's key in on this just to make sure were all on the same page.

So - If you have any proof to back up your claims - make sure you utilize it!

Just to name a few common examples:

- Let's say you made a deal with a debt collector, and the debt collector agreed to delete the account from your report but failed to do so after it was paid. Make sure you include a copy of the agreement.

- Or maybe you were a victim of identity theft and you have a police report, definitely include a copy.

- Sometimes creditors make mistakes, if you have any letters that say it - use it.

- I've seen situations where people had cancelled checks for paid debts still appearing as unpaid on their reports - this is credit repair gold! You should absolutely insert copies with the dispute letters!

If you have any proof, this would be the time to print it and include it in your envelope.

Mailing Your Letters

Now it's time to mail the letters to the 3 credit bureaus. I have included a downloadable PDF with the addresses for each of the credit bureaus, but remember - if you are using Credit Repair Cloud software, all of this information is automatically populated into the letters for you!

After you print out your first round of letters, simply include your government issued ID and a utility bill in each envelope and drop in the mail.

Waiting Period

So, now that you've mailed your Round 1 Letters, you are waiting for the 3 bureaus to respond. Technically, the bureaus have 30 days from the date they receive your letters to respond, which could take a few days from the time you mailed them for the bureaus to receive and process them.

Then their investigation begins. They will contact the source of the information that you disputed and generally speaking, they usually do this pretty quickly. When their done, they will mail you the results. There will be a couple of days before the mail arrives back to you. Although the process is generally quick and usually takes under 30 days, don't be surprised if it takes up to 45 days to receive everything back from the credit bureaus.

With the credit repair process, most of your time is spent waiting for results.

Results

When the results finally arrive, they arrive individually - one from each of the 3 credit bureaus (Experian, Equifax and TransUnion. Typically each letter is in 10in X 8in plain white unmarked envelope. If you're working with a client, be sure to have them forward these responses to you.

When you open the envelopes, usually you will find one of two things:

1. A stall letter OR
2. an actual investigation.

If its a stall letter, read it and based on it's contents you can figure out what to do next.

If its an investigation result - it generally will look like this:

1. A couple pages of consumer disclosures advising you of your rights.
2. A blank page, intentionally left blank.
3. A full or partial credit report.
4. An investigation results page, listing the accounts which were investigated, along with the outcome of each investigation.

The latter, the investigation results page is what you're looking for. We are going to dig a little deeper on this in the next lesson.

Lesson #6 **Beyond Round 1**

Ok so you've sent out your round one letters, now what?

For starters, expect each of the 3 bureaus to mail you a response, but also expect some pushback. This is totally normal. One or more of the credit bureaus may fail to respond or respond with a stall letter.
- How do you handle those situations?
- What if the credit bureaus verify the information is accurate, what do you do then?
- What letters do you send?
- How often do you send them?

I will explain all of this to you in this lesson plus much more.

Common Responses

The FCRA requires the credit bureaus and sometimes the furnisher to send a written response, depending on the situation - but for the most part, you should always expect a response.

Typically, each credit bureau will send you either a full credit report or partial report with a cover page that summarizes the changes. Generally they are easy to read and understand. The responses are important because it lets you know whether or not the disputed information was modified or removed, but it also provides important clues. Deciphering the responses may seem complicated but it's really not.

We're going to start by talking about Credit Bureau Responses.

The credit bureaus (Equifax, Experian and TransUnion) have developed a system of stalling the credit repair process and discouraging consumers from repairing their credit. Some of the stall tactics include sending letters designed to make you believe they wont do what you want.

Some of the most common stall letters are:

- A letter saying they received a suspicious request to access your credit file.
- A letter stating that the request you sent them was not legible
- They may say they require additional documents to verify your identity
- Another very common response is "Your request was deemed frivolous and will NOT be investigated."

When you are faced with such disappointing responses, many people simply give up. (DONT!)

You should expect these response at some point during the process, the credit bureaus will use these tactics, so be ready for them. When your faced with a stall tactic, leverage your rights and aggressively re-initiate the investigation. The course your taking today is a Basic Disputing Course, so I will not be going over every scenario, but what I can tell you is that here at

Credit Repair Cloud, we have over 100 letters, training, support and an amazing community of credit experts that will help you tackle any situation.

Although many of the responses you receive will be designed to discourage you, you will also be surprised at how the bureaus often delete items, sometimes items you would think would be difficult just fall off.

When it comes to Furnisher responses, it's common for a furnisher to respond to a dispute asking for more information or evidence the account is incorrect. They often use similar stall tactics just like the credit bureaus.

You can expect vague responses, often no response at all - but again, this is where you can leverage your rights as a consumer.

For example, if a furnisher doesn't respond to a simple dispute letter - you can demand validation. When you do this, it places the burden of proof on the furnisher to supply you with actual proof the account is correct. You may receive a simple letter saying the account is valid, you or may receive a massive envelope with your original contract and copies of every account statement going back 10 years.

So with that being said, you can expect a wide range of responses from the furnishers.

3 Primary Categories

The next step you take depends on the response you received. There are many ways it can go... But for the sake of simplicity, I have categorized all of the different response types into 3 primary categories:

1. **No Response:** meaning you do not receive any response in the mail.

2. **Verified:** meaning, the bureau refuses to delete them. This could be a verification letter, or a stall letter or a request for more information, regardless of the details - we categorize this as Verified.

3. **Deleted:** this is the result you want - the bureau removed the information from your report!

It's very important that you understand how to handle responses correctly because it these quick little decisions will play a huge role in your overall success.

NO RESPONSE: If a credit bureau fails to respond to a dispute you sent, for example of the 3 letters you sent, Experian doesn't respond... It's ok, don't take it personally - you should always simply follow up by using the "No Response" letter template. This will usually get their attention without having to make any threats. So, again, whenever a credit bureau simply fails to respond to your round 1 letter - just fill out the "No Response" letter template and drop it in the mail.

VERIFIED: Next, let's say that Equifax responds to the letter you mailed them and verifies the information refusing to delete it. That's ok, the key here is persistence. Don't take no for an answer - ever! In this situation, simply use the "Reinvestigation" letter, change the text as you see fit and drop it in your mailbox. Easy.

DELETED: Finally, it is very possible you get good news back, TransUnion deleted some or all of the items you disputed... AWESOME! What do you do next: You should dispute more items using the same exact Round 1 letter! Yup, start over at the beginning and challenge more items!

Remember, every cycle will be different. Each credit bureau maintains their own records and has different procedures, so you will often see items removed on one bureau, but not the next. It can become complicated keeping track of all of the results. Those of you taking advantage of the Credit Repair Cloud software, don't really need to worry about this. The system makes it super easy to keep track of everything.

So, now you know what the responses "no response", "verified" and "deleted" mean and how to respond, so send out your follow up letters and wait another 30 days.

Responses from Round 1

This is where we left off on the dispute process chart, we sent round 1. Now, you need to identify the outcome from the first round. Take a look at the responses. Each of the 3 bureaus should have sent you a letter.

1. **NO RESPONSE:** If any of them failed to do this, you now need to send Letter #2 "The No Response letter"

2. **VERIFIED:** If any of the credit bureaus verified the items you disputed, you should send Letter #3 "The Reinvestigation Letter"

3. **DELETED:** What if the credit bureau deleted all the items? Awesome! You can go back and dispute more items using the same Round #1 Letter.

It's really that simple.

Follow Up with the Credit Bureaus

I'm including a full image of Round 2 so you can start connecting the dots. Now that you've sent your follow up letters, you can see this cycle is JUST LIKE like the last cycle. You look at the responses and determine what to do next, you fire off your next cycle of letters, then you wait for the next round of responses.

Send a Warning Shot

So at this point, you sent a Round 1 letter and depending on the results you received - or lack thereof, you have either sent a "No response" letter or a "Reinvestigation" letter.

When you get the next round of results, just like last time - inspect them. If you got a bunch of deletions - AWESOME. Just like before, you can always revert back to Round 1 and dispute more items. But, if that's not the case and the credit bureaus are still ignoring you, or responding inappropriately, it's time to send a warning shot. The bureau warning letter is a bit more aggressive - making it very clear that you mean business. So, if that's the case, go ahead and fire off a warning letter to each bureau that is not taking you seriously.

Furnisher Disputes

We just talked about disputing with the credit bureaus. As I said before, I'll say it again: persistence pays. The process of disputing items with the bureaus can be repeated as many times as you like.

Often, when you least expect it; even when you have disputed an item 10 times - all of the sudden on the 11th attempt it magically disappears! So don't give up - but also consider other options such as furnisher disputes.

When you have exhausted your efforts with the bureaus and progress seems to have slowed down, the next step is to contact the companies that reported the negative information - these are called furnishers.

Furnishers can be creditors like credit card companies, banks, lenders or collection agencies. There are many others such as landlords, child support courts, bankruptcy court and more.

Anyone that reported information about you is a furnisher and subject to the same laws and... many of the laws that regulate the credit bureaus also regulate the furnishers, in some cases the laws are even more stringent.

Go ahead and send letter #5 "Dispute with Furnisher" and just like you did on the first step with the credit bureaus, you will include a reason and instruction for each item you are disputing. Easy peasy, fill in the blanks and fire off your first letters. You can send a letter to some or all of your furnishers, that is really up to you. You will then sit back and relax while you wait for the results.

Follow Up with Furnishers

After 30 days or so, review the responses. Just like we did with the credit bureaus, we are looking for the results of each investigation. Look to see what was received and determine if the furnishers responded, verified or deleted the items you disputed.

- If no response was received from any of furnishers, go ahead and use Letter #6, No Response.
- If any of the furnishers verified the item you disputed, go ahead and send letter #7, Reinvestigation.
- If the furnisher deleted the item, awesome! You can dispute more items using the same old letter #5, Dispute with Furnisher.

Drop your letters in the mail and wait for the results.

Results from Furnisher Follow Up

I'm including a full image of Round 5 so you can connect the dots. Now that you've sent your follow up letters to the furnishers, you can see this cycle is JUST LIKE the last cycle. Look at the responses from your follow up letters and determine what to do next. What was the response? Verified, no response or deleted?

Send a Warning Shot

If the furnisher deleted everything, that's great - you can go back again and send Letter #5, Dispute with Furnisher and challenge some more items. If the furnishers verified the items or failed to respond - it's time to take your warning shot! Let them know you mean business and send Letter #8, Creditor Warning letters to each of the furnishers that did not respond with a deletion. Send out your warning letters, and wait for a response.

Demand Validation

So far, you have disputed items with the bureaus, followed up with them and sent a warning. If that didn't work, you switched gears and sent disputes to furnishers, followed up and sent warnings the creditors or debt collection agencies. If that doesn't get the items deleted, there are still plenty of strategies to keep keep chipping away to get them removed. Although this is a "basic disputing course" I am starting to move into advanced waters, - but I would like to offer at least two more options for you at this stage.

Now that you sent warnings to the furnishers that either did not respond or did not delete what you asked, the next step would be to demand validation. Debt validation is typically only used on debt collection agencies, unless your state law provides otherwise, the FDCPA only requires debt collectors, not original creditors, to verify debts. You still can always try even if it is not a 3rd party debt collector.

The right to request verification of the debt is provided by the federal Fair Debt Collection Practices Act (FDCPA). The law was enacted to allow consumers to obtain more information about the debt that is being collected and to act as an informal dispute resolution system between consumers and their collectors.

There are many instances when you may want to request verification of the debt. Some may include:

- Perhaps you don't recognize or remember incurring the debt being collected.
- You may feel that the amount of the debt may not be correct.
- Maybe the debt is expired or not yours at all.

You want to verify that the collector actually owns the debt it is trying to collect. Even if you have no reason to contest the validity of the debt, the FDCPA still allows you to request verification. This means that even if the debt is legitimately yours and is owed, you still have a right to request verification. A debt collector may not ask you to cite reasons why you want verification of the debt.

So, go ahead and give it a whirl. Send Letter #9 Validation Demand and wait 30 days.

Send Estoppel

So you've sent a validation letter to the furnishers that either ignored or verified your previous disputes. Your next step depends on the response from the furnishers. Did they delete the item from your report? If yes, GREAT! You can dispute more items using letter #5.

Did they ignore your validation demand?

If yes, the next logical step would be to send Letter #10 - Estoppel by Silence. This is a letter that can be extremely powerful when debt collectors ignore a request for verification. Essentially it tells the collection agency that by being silent, they must agree with you. So, if you reach this point and the debt collectors ignore your validation demand, go ahead and fill out the Estoppel By Silence Letter #10 and mail it out.

Start Over

So what comes next? Just like every other round, it depends on the responses you receive.

Throughout this course, I have articulated some of the most basic strategies and scenarios. By now, you should be able to put a finger on 90% of the process, but just like anything in life - the more you put into something, the more you get out of it. The best way to level up and truly understand credit repair, is to do it yourself.

You've run the basic disputing options full course - at this point you have the option to either start over from the beginning with Letter #1 and dispute again with the credit bureaus or use letter #5 and dispute with the furnishers.

There are also many additional strategies and advanced options you can learn.

Be Persistent & Apply Pressure

It appears we've gone full circle. At this point, you should have a fundamental understanding of the credit system and the laws that can be used to your advantage as well as some of the basic strategies to repair your credit.

- With credit repair – you've got to be persistent and apply pressure every step of the way!
- Whatever you do, make sure you do not take the responses or lack thereof personally.
- The bureaus will usually do everything within their power to convince you that your efforts are in vain.
- Never give up when you encounter resistance – just keep applying pressure.

Think of credit repair as a little bit of work, every once in awhile over a long period of time, 99.99% of the time is waiting for mail to arrive.

- Some people with minimal problems, or people that have proof finish very quickly.
- Many people that have major problems follow the process I've outlined in this course and are able to move mountains quickly - sometimes getting all the items they dispute deleted on the first try.
- But the majority of credit repair requires you to fight a bit. So again, whatever you do - never give up!

You Got This

Whether you are repairing your credit for yourself or helping a friend, family member or maybe you want to build a credit repair empire, either way - you've got this! You can do it!

I gotta mention one more time that Credit Repair Cloud makes the process much, much easier.

Everything from importing and auditing the credit reports with one click to automatically generating the letters and keeping track of the results, it literally makes everything a breeze - so easy you can do this in your sleep.

We have made it not only easy and fast to get your business off the ground - we give you an actual blueprint and every tool you could possibly need, to become the next credit repair millionaire, like these guys here!

Thousands of credit repair companies are using our software and many have become millionaires. By the way, most of the people in our millionaires club did not come from money or even a business background. Many didn't even go to college. They learned credit repair by repairing their own credit after facing their own financial hardships. But when they started helping family and friends, and felt the satisfaction that you feel when you're changing someone's life, they were hooked. It's that desire to help people that makes them so successful. If you set out to make money, sure you'll make money, but you probably won't have a very fulfilling life. But when you set out to help people and truly change lives, that is when you will have the greatest success.

Congrats! You've made it through the entire course.

Credit Bureau Contact Information

Experian
P.O. Box 9701
Allen, TX 75013
(888) 397-3742
www.experian.com

Equifax
P.O. Box 740256
Atlanta, GA 30374
(866) 349-5191
www.equifax.com

TransUnion
P.O. Box 2000
Chester, PA 19022
(800) 916-8800
www.transunion.com

77

Top 10 Basic Dispute Letters

The following letters are included as "Bonus Items" in this course which can be found in the "Top 10 Letter Booklet" and also the Zip File labeled "Top 10 Letter Templates" so you can use if you want to do credit repair the hard way - without our amazing software!

Letter #1 – "Default Round 1 (Dispute Credit Report Items)"

DESCRIPTION: Round #1 letter is typically the first letter you send to the bureaus and can be used to request verification, the bureaus will contact the furnishers to verify or remove unverifiable items from credit report.

IMPORTANT: The text in brackets "{example}" are placeholders that must be modified by you. If you are using Credit Repair Cloud software, the information is automatically inserted into the letter for you. If you are not using our software, make sure you delete these instructions and replace the text.

* THIS LETTER IS INCLUDED IN THE CREDIT REPAIR CLOUD LETTER LIBRARY *

************************* ^ DELETE TITLE & INSTRUCTIONS ABOVE ^ *************************

{client_first_name} {client_last_name}
{client_address}
{bdate}

{ss_number}

{bureau_address}

{curr_date}

Re: Letter to Remove Inaccurate Credit Information

To Whom It May Concern:
I received a copy of my credit report and found the following item(s) to be in error:

{Creditor/Collector Name + Account Number + Reason + Instruction}

By the provisions of the Fair Credit Reporting Act, I demand that these items be investigated and removed from my report. It is my understanding that you will recheck these items with the creditor who has posted them. Please remove any information that the creditor cannot verify. I understand that under 15 U.S.C. Sec.

1681i(a), you must complete this reinvestigation within 30 days of receipt of this letter.

Please send an updated copy of my credit report to the above address. According to the act, there shall be no charge for this updated report. I also request that you please send notices of corrections to anyone who received my credit report in the past six months.

Thank you for your time and help in this matter.

Sincerely,
{client_signature}
_____
{client_first_name} {client_last_name}

Letter #2 – "Bureau No Response"

Description: Use this letter to remind the credit bureau to respond when round one is ignored.

IMPORTANT: The text in brackets "{example}" are placeholders that must be modified by you. If you are using Credit Repair Cloud software, the information is automatically inserted into the letter for you. If you are not using our software, make sure you delete these instructions and replace the text.

* THIS LETTER IS INCLUDED IN THE CREDIT REPAIR CLOUD LETTER LIBRARY *

*************************** ^ DELETE TITLE & INSTRUCTIONS ABOVE ^ *************************

{client_first_name} {client_last_name}
{client_address}
{bdate}
{ss_number}

{bureau_address}

{curr_date}

To Whom It May Concern,
This letter is a formal complaint that you have ignored my previous request and failed to maintain reasonable procedures in your operations to assure maximum possible accuracy in the credit reports you publish. Credit reporting laws ensure that bureaus report only 100% accurate credit information and every step must be taken to assure the information reported is completely accurate and correct.
Please refer to my previous letter for the information that needs to be re-investigated.

{Creditor/Collector Name + Account Number + Reason + Instruction}

The information must be deleted from my report as soon as possible. The information is inaccurate and misleading and as such represents a very serious error in your reporting.

Under federal law, you have thirty (30) days to complete your re-investigation. Be advised that the description of the procedure used to determine the accuracy and completeness of the information is hereby requested as well, to be provided within fifteen (15) days of the completion of your re-investigation.

Sincerely yours,
{client_signature}

_____
{client_first_name} {client_last_name}

Letter #3 – "Bureau Re-Investigation"

DESCRIPTION: 60 day follow up demand to credit bureau with warning to re-investigate disputed items.

IMPORTANT: The text in brackets "{example}" are placeholders that must be modified by you. If you are using Credit Repair Cloud software, the information is automatically inserted into the letter for you. If you are not using our software, make sure you delete these instructions and replace the text.

* THIS LETTER IS INCLUDED IN THE CREDIT REPAIR CLOUD LETTER LIBRARY *

*************************** ^ DELETE TITLE & INSTRUCTIONS ABOVE ^ ***************************

{client_first_name} {client_last_name}
{client_address}
{bdate}
{ss_number}

{bureau_address}

Attn: Customer Relations Department

{curr_date}

To Whom It May Concern,
I am in total disagreement with your investigation response. The incorrect items listed below still appear on my credit report, even after your investigation. I would like these items immediately re-investigated and for good cause. These inaccuracies are highly injurious to my credit rating.

{Creditor/Collector Name + Account Number + Reason + Instruction}

Furthermore, In accordance with The Fair Credit Reporting Act, Public law 91-506, Title VI, Section 611, Subsection A-D, I demand that you provide actual proof the information was verified, not a computer generated confirmation.

Please provide:

1. The names and business addresses of each individual with whom you verified the information with above, so that I may follow up.
2. The date you contacted the individual furnisher's information.
3. The method of communication you used to verify the information

I would also like to know if the furnisher provided you with my SSN, address or DOB.
Please forward an updated credit report to me after you have completed your investigation and corrections.

Your cooperation and prompt attention are required by law.

Sincerely,

{client_signature}

_____
{client_first_name} {client_last_name}

Letter #4 – "Bureau Warning"

DESCRIPTION: Follow up demand to credit bureau with stern warning to re-investigate disputed items.

IMPORTANT: The text in brackets "{example}" are placeholders that must be modified by you. If you are using Credit Repair Cloud software, the information is automatically inserted into the letter for you. If you are not using our software, make sure you delete these instructions and replace the text.

* THIS LETTER IS INCLUDED IN THE CREDIT REPAIR CLOUD LETTER LIBRARY *

*************************** ^ DELETE TITLE & INSTRUCTIONS ABOVE ^ ***************************

{client_first_name} {client_last_name}
{client_address}
{bdate}
{ss_number}

{bureau_address}

Re: Warning to Remove Incorrect Items from my Credit Report

{curr_date}

To Whom It May Concern:

I recently sent you a request to reinvestigate the information previously disputed. I have attached my previous correspondence for you to revisit.

The computer-generated response I received is unacceptable and I am losing patience. If the information is not immediately reinvestigated and removed, I will be forced to seek legal counsel for relief through the court and file complaints with regulatory enforcement agencies including the CFPB, FTC and my state attorney general.

Remove this incorrect information at once and send me an updated copy of my credit history report.

{Creditor/Collector Name + Account Number + Reason + Instruction}
I also request that you please send notices of corrections to anyone who received my credit report in the past six months.

Sincerely,
{client_signature}

_____
{client_first_name} {client_last_name}

Letter #5 – "Furnisher Basic Dispute"

DESCRIPTION: The first letter you send to furnishers and can be used to request verification.

IMPORTANT: The text in brackets "{example}" are placeholders that must be modified by you. If you are using Credit Repair Cloud software, the information is automatically inserted into the letter for you. If you are not using our software, make sure you delete these instructions and replace the text.

* THIS LETTER IS INCLUDED IN THE CREDIT REPAIR CLOUD LETTER LIBRARY *

************************* ^ DELETE TITLE & INSTRUCTIONS ABOVE ^ *************************

{client_first_name} {client_last_name}
{client_address}
{ss_number}

{creditor_name}
{creditor_address}
{creditor_city}, {creditor_state} {creditor_zip}

Re: Remove Inaccurate Information from my Credit Reports.

{curr_date}

To Whom It May Concern:

I received a copy of my credit report and found you are reporting incorrect information to the credit bureaus.

Here are the error(s):

{Creditor/Collector Name + Account Number + Reason + Instruction}

Under federal law, as a furnisher of information to consumer reporting agencies, you must conduct a reasonable investigation of my dispute and you must complete this investigation within 30 days of receipt of this letter. I demand that this information be investigated and either verified or removed from my report.

Please send me confirmation the information has been removed from my credit files.

Thank you for your time and help in this matter.

Sincerely,

{client_signature}

_____
{client_first_name} {client_last_name}

Letter #6 – "Furnisher No Response"

DESCRIPTION: 30 Day reminder to furnisher to respond when basic dispute is ignored.

IMPORTANT: The text in brackets "{example}" are placeholders that must be modified by you. If you are using Credit Repair Cloud software, the information is automatically inserted into the letter for you. If you are not using our software, make sure you delete these instructions and replace the text.

* THIS LETTER IS INCLUDED IN THE CREDIT REPAIR CLOUD LETTER LIBRARY *

************************** ^ DELETE TITLE & INSTRUCTIONS ABOVE ^ **************************

{client_first_name} {client_last_name}
{client_address}
{bdate}
{ss_number}

{creditor_name}
{creditor_address}
{creditor_city}, {creditor_state} {creditor_zip}

{curr_date}

To Whom It May Concern,
This letter is a formal complaint that you have reported inaccurate and incomplete credit information to the credit bureaus.

Federal laws require furnishers of information to report accurate credit information to the credit bureaus and in this case, you have failed to do so. Every step must be taken to assure the information reported is completely accurate and correct. I disputed the following information over 30 days ago and you have not yet responded:

{Creditor/Collector Name + Account Number + Reason + Instruction}

This inaccurate information must be deleted from my credit file immediately. Please contact the credit agencies you have reported it to and remove this misleading information from my credit profile.

Under federal law, you must complete your re-investigation in a timely manner. Be advised that the description of the procedure used to determine the accuracy and completeness of the information is hereby requested as well, to be provided within fifteen (15) days of the completion of your investigation.

Sincerely yours,
{client_signature}

_____
{client_first_name} {client_last_name}

Letter #7 – "Furnisher Re-investigation"

DESCRIPTION: 60 day follow up demand to furnisher with request to re-investigate disputed items.

IMPORTANT: The text in brackets "{example}" are placeholders that must be modified by you. If you are using Credit Repair Cloud software, the information is automatically inserted into the letter for you. If you are not using our software, make sure you delete these instructions and replace the text.

*************************** ^ DELETE TITLE & INSTRUCTIONS ABOVE ^ ***************************

{client_first_name} {client_last_name}
{client_address}
{bdate}
{ss_number}

{creditor_name}
{creditor_address}
{creditor_city}, {creditor_state} {creditor_zip}

Attn: Customer Relations Department

{curr_date}

To Whom It May Concern,

I am in disagreement with the information listed below which you reported to the credit agencies and still appear on my credit report, even after your investigation. I would like these item(s) immediately re-investigated and removed. These inaccuracies are impacting my credit rating.

{Creditor/Collector Name + Account Number + Reason + Instruction}

Please confirm you have completed your investigation and corrections by notifying by mail. Your cooperation and prompt attention are appreciated.

Sincerely yours,

{client_signature}
_____
{client_first_name} {client_last_name}

Letter #8 – "Furnisher Warning"

DESCRIPTION: Follow up demand to furnisher with stern warning to re-investigate disputed items.

IMPORTANT: The text in brackets "{example}" are placeholders that must be modified by you. If you are using Credit Repair Cloud software, the information is automatically inserted into the letter for you. If you are not using our software, make sure you delete these instructions and replace the text.

************************** ^ DELETE TITLE & INSTRUCTIONS ABOVE ^ **************************

{client_first_name} {client_last_name}
{client_address}
{bdate}
{ss_number}

{creditor_name}
{creditor_address}
{creditor_city}, {creditor_state} {creditor_zip}

Re: Warning

{curr_date}

To Whom It May Concern:

I recently sent you a request to reinvestigate incorrect items which you reported to the credit agencies. You ignored my request.

Federal law requires that you complete your reinvestigation of my request within 30 days. It has now been more than 30 days and the items remain on my report:

{Creditor/Collector Name + Account Number + Reason + Instruction}

I will assume that I have not received your reply because you have been unable to verify this information. If the information is not immediately reinvestigated and removed, I will be forced to seek legal counsel for relief through the court and file complaints with regulatory enforcement agencies including the CFPB, FTC and my state attorney general.

Sincerely yours,

{client_signature}

_____
{client_first_name} {client_last_name}

Letter #9 – "Validation"

{client_first_name} {client_last_name}
{client_address}

{creditor_name}
{creditor_address}
{creditor_city}, {creditor_state} {creditor_zip}

RE: Validation Required

{curr_date}

Re: Account # {account_number}

To Whom It May Concern,

I dispute your claim and I am requesting validation from you pursuant to the Fair Debt Collection Practices Act, 15 USC 1692g Sec. 809 (8) (FDCPA).

- Provide breakdown of fees including how you calculated what you claim I owe. 2 Provide a copy of my signature on a contract or document that holds me responsible for this alleged debt.
- Cease any credit bureau reporting until debt has been validated by me as required under the FCRA.
- Send me proof that you are licensed to collect debt in my state.

- Send this information to my address listed above and accept this letter-sent as my formal debt validation request, which I am allowed under the FDCPA.

I will await your reply with above requested proof. Upon receiving it, I will correspond back with you.

Sincerely,

{client_signature}
_____
{client_first_name}{client_last_name}

Letter #10 – "Estoppel By Silence"

DESCRIPTION: Demand reinvestigation and validation demand to collection agency, failure warning using estoppel.

IMPORTANT: The text in brackets "{example}" are placeholders that must be modified by you. If you are using Credit Repair Cloud software, the information is automatically inserted into the letter for you. If you are not using our software, make sure you delete these instructions and replace the text.

* THIS LETTER IS INCLUDED IN THE CREDIT REPAIR CLOUD LETTER LIBRARY *

************************ ^ DELETE TITLE & INSTRUCTIONS ABOVE ^ ************************

{client_first_name} {client_last_name}
{client_address}

{creditor_name}
{creditor_address}
{creditor_city}, {creditor_state} {creditor_zip}

{curr_date}

Re: Account number: {account_number}

To Whom It May Concern:
This letter is to formally advise you that I believe your company has violated several of my consumer rights. Specifically, you failed to validate a debt at my request, which is an FDCPA violation and you continued to report a disputed debt to the Credit Bureaus: another FCRA violation. Not only have you ignored my prior requests for validation of debt (proof attached: receipt copies or letter copies) but you continue to report this debt to the credit bureaus causing damage to my character.

This letter will again request that you follow the FDCPA and please provide the following validation of debt request:

- Proof of your right to own/collect this alleged debt
- Balance claimed including all fees, interest and penalties

- Contract bearing my personal signature

As you may be aware, "Estoppel by Silence" legally means that you had a duty to speak but failed to do so therefore, that must mean you agree with me that this debt is false. I will use the Estoppel in my defense.

I expect to receive the proof requested above within 15 days of this letter. Should you again ignore my request for validation of debt I reserve the right to sue your company for violation of my consumer rights as specified under both the FDCPA and the FCRA. I may also seek damages from you if warranted.

Kind regards,
{client_signature}

_____

{client_first_name} {client_last_name}

GLOSSARY

A

ASU (Accident, Sickness, and Unemployment Insurance) – Also known as ASR (Accident, Sickness, and Redundancy Insurance). ASU protects borrowers against the financial consequences of being unable to work for the reasons detailed in the policy. Different companies charge different premiums for ASU, and policy terms may vary as well. The policy covers a portion of the consumer's mortgage, insurance, and income for a limited amount of time (for either six months or a year, in some cases, or until the borrower returns to work).

Account Number – Accounts have account numbers to uniquely identify them individually. As it relates to credit cards, all cardholder accounts feature a unique account number composed of 16 digits. Each digit represents specific information on your card. The first six digits convey the issuer identification number, while the seventh through the second-to-last digits refer to your personal account number. Generated through what is called the Luhn formula, the final digit is called the "checksum" or "check digit."

Activate – Many card issuers ask you to call them in order to activate your new card, with the aim of confirming that the approved cardholder has the card in their possession. Some card issuers allow you to activate your card online, using your Online Banking ID and passcode.

Activity – Activity refers to the transactions on your statement each billing cycle (i.e., payments, purchases, fees, finance charges, and more).

Additional Cardholder – Many consumers choose to add a second cardholder to their account (most often a spouse). Some accounts feature more than two cardholders. As a cardholder, you are liable for the charges incurred on the account.

Administration Fee – Many lenders charge a nonrefundable fee to cover administrative costs if the borrower's mortgage application falls through. While this fee is frequently included in the valuation fee, the applicant must still pay the administration fee if the valuation does not take place. Administration fees are also known as application fees.

Advance-Fee Loan – An illegitimate loan in which the borrower is asked to pay a fee upfront and receive a substantial sum with a low annual percentage rate. Fees are not prominently disclosed in advance-fee loans. These are also known as Payday Advances.

Affidavit – A verified written document made by a person under oath. These statements must be notarized.

Affinity Card – A credit card issued by a standard card issuer in partnership with a non-bank entity such as a charitable organization. Whenever a purchase is made, a percentage of the transaction goes to the non-bank entity.

Agreement – A contract provided by the card issuer detailing the terms that apply to the card in question. Terms list transaction fees, interest rates, and the methods used to determine these figures. Consumers should avoid working with card issuers who do not disclose the full terms of the agreement before you are asked to sign the contract.

Amortization – Paying off a debt in installments of principal and earned interest over a specific period of time.

Amount Due – Most often your minimum monthly credit card payment rather than your total outstanding balance.

Annual Fee – A yearly fee some card issuers may charge to your account.

Annual Review – A review of your account to determine future changes. Your interest rate may change year upon year, depending on how the card issuer calculated your base rate the year before.

Applicant – A consumer applying for credit privileges, a loan, or employment.

Appraisal Fee – The cost of hiring a professional appraiser to evaluate the market value of your home.

Appreciation – The result of a changing market, or for some consumers, home improvements and other renovations. The market value of your home will likely go up—or appreciate—over time.

APR – Annual percentage rate. Consumers can divide their APR by 12 to calculate what they owe in interest each month. For example, an APR of 24% would translate to a 2% monthly interest rate.

Arrangement Fee – Charged for consumers to access specific deals on their mortgages (in particular fixed- or discounted-rate mortgage deals). Some arrangement fees are payable upfront, while others are added or subtracted at the end of the loan's term. Contact your lender for more information.

Arrears – Outstanding mortgage payments that are now past due. Borrowers with arrears on their mortgage may struggle to find a new mortgage through a conventional lender. Some lenders, however, specialize in consumers with arrears.

ATM – Automated teller machine. ATMs allow consumers to make monetary deposits and withdrawals—in addition to transfers and other inquiries—in a convenient manner. Some ATM transactions include fees from more than one bank. Others may include fees based on location, or on the type of ATM.

Authorization – Permission to complete a transaction from the card issuer. Different businesses impose different limits on the funds consumers can spend via credit card without seeking authorization. The idea here is to keep cardholders from going over their credit limit, and to identify fraud. Note that authorization can be done electronically or by phone at the time your card is swiped. You may in some cases need to verify your identity before the purchase goes through.

Authorized User – Individuals who have been granted permission by the approved cardholder to use the liable party's credit card. Authorized users differ from joint account holders, in which both parties are obliged to pay. In some cases, the authorized user will receive a credit card in his or her name, even though it is linked to someone else's account. Also see "Piggybacking".

Automatic Payment – An automatic transfer made from a bank account to pay a credit card bill. The account must come from the bank that issued the card. The idea is to minimize the risk of late payments and additional fees.

Available Credit – Credit you have not yet used within your credit limit in the current billing cycle.

Average Daily Balance – Calculated by taking the sum of your outstanding balance for each day in the billing period, and then dividing that figure by the total number of days in the billing cycle. Your average daily balance is used to calculate new payments and purchases, and other finance charges.

B

Bad Credit – A negative credit rating reflected in your FICO score and credit history. Consumers who make late payments or skip payments altogether, among other behaviors, may experience poor credit. Those with bad credit tend to struggle getting approved for credit from traditional lenders.

Balance – Money currently owed that you have not yet paid. Your balance is different than your monthly payment, as it is the total money owed at that time rather than the minimum payment. Your balance may include unpaid bills, advances, purchases charged on your card, and any interest you must pay.

Balance Transfer – Moving a debt to another credit card. This is typically done to transfer a long-term debt to an account with lower interest so that you can pay the debt down faster. Contact your card issuer or look at your card agreement to determine how you can initiate a balance transfer.

Balloon Payment – A substantial payment due at the end of a balloon loan. Balloon payments are typically the repayment of the principal sum you put down initially.

Bankruptcy – A voluntary or involuntary process in which a business petitions the federal court because they can no longer pay down their debts. In bankruptcy, either the debtor's liabilities are reorganized or their assets are liquidated.

Bankruptcy Chapter 7 – The liquidation of the debtor's assets such that the debtor can eliminate their debt by giving up property unprotected by exemption laws. A bankruptcy trustee can then distribute the funds to creditors. Any remaining unpaid debt will be wiped out. A Chapter 7 bankruptcy may be listed on the debtor's credit report for up to a decade. Detailed under the Federal Bankruptcy Code.

Bankruptcy Chapter 11 – Business reorganization rather than the liquidation of assets. The debtor will propose a repayment plan. Once the plan is approved, they can begin paying off their creditors. A Chapter 11 bankruptcy may be listed on the debtor's credit report for up to a decade. Detailed under the Federal Bankruptcy Code.

Bankruptcy Chapter 12 – Reorganization for fishermen and farmers to avoid liquidation and foreclosure. A Chapter 12 bankruptcy may be listed on the debtor's credit report for up to seven years. Detailed under the Federal Bankruptcy Code.

Bankruptcy Chapter 13 – Business reorganization rather than the liquidation of assets. The debtor will propose a repayment plan. Once the plan is approved, they can begin paying off their creditors. Unlike a Chapter 11 bankruptcy proceeding, only debtors with a stable income can file a Chapter 13 bankruptcy; for this reason, a Chapter 13 bankruptcy proceeding is often called a "wage earner plan." This bankruptcy chapter may be listed on the debtor's credit report for up to seven years if it is discharged, or 10 years if it is not discharged. Detailed under the Federal Bankruptcy Code.

Bankruptcy Discharged – A court order releasing the debtor from their obligation to pay a debt after completing the requirements for their case.

Bankruptcy Dismissed – A court order denying the debtor's petition to file bankruptcy. The debtor will liable for their debt as a result of a dismissal.

Bill – A written report detailing your account activity for the previous billing cycle, including what you owe. The reverse side of the bill features the terms of your card agreement and additional information (i.e., your card issuer's contact information and methods used to calculate interest or other fees). Bills are typically sent at the end of each month.

Billing Cycle – The period of time between billings—typically 20 to 45 days depending on the credit card or the card issuer.

Bond - As it relates to the credit repair industry, a bond is a type of surety bond that ensures the principal of the credit repair company will abide by all applicable rules and regulations. The bond provides protection for the obligee (the entity requiring the bond) and consumers in the event of misconduct by the credit repair company.

Borrower – An individual or organization making a purchase with borrowed money (that is, the money of another person or entity). Also known as a "debtor."

Budget – A financial plan or itemized list of expenses consumers use to record their saving and spending habits. Some consumers create a budget to track how their expenses compare to their income.

Budget Card – A prepaid card consumers use by making monthly payments via direct debit to cover past and future purchases.

Building Insurance – Protects the lender and the borrower in the event that the building they own collapses or becomes damaged. Many lenders include building insurance in the mortgage.

Buydown – A mortgage-financing strategy in which the borrower pays a lump sum to the creditor in order to get a lower interest rate at the beginning of the mortgage term.

C

Capacity – The ability to make on-time mortgage payments. A product of the borrower's income, assets, and expenses. Lenders also take into account the funds the borrower has left over after covering their monthly debt obligations.

Capital – The consumer's savings, assets, and investments—anything they own of monetary value. Cash reserves are a form of liquid capital.

Cash Advance – A loan consumers receive by using their cards at a bank or ATM. Cash loans feature higher interest rates than standard purchases, and have minimal flexibility. Note that you may incur a handling fee for taking out a cash advance, along with other hidden costs.

Cash Back (on Credit Cards) – Cash rewards the consumer receives as a result of using their credit card. Card issuers pay back a portion of what the consumer spends on their card at the end of the month or year.

Cash Back (on Mortgages) – Money the lender gives back to the borrower in cash at the beginning of the mortgage. The total sum may vary; borrowers who agree to pay the normal variable mortgage rate rather than a fixed or discounted rate typically receive the most cash back. Contact your lender for more information, as Capital Gains Tax may apply. Many lenders also charge early redemption penalties for borrowers who pay off their mortgage early, so keep this in mind before you sign your contract.

CCCS (Consumer Credit Counseling Services) - CCCS stands for Consumer Credit Counseling Services. Each CCCS agency offers a common set of services, including financial education, budgeting assistance, and Debt Management Plans.

CFPB (Consumer Financial Protection Bureau) The Consumer Financial Protection Bureau is an agency of the United States government responsible for consumer protection in the financial sector. When disputing with the bureaus or furnishers, filing complaints with the CFPB is a common credit repair tactic.

Charge Card – A card with an account that must be paid in full when you receive your statement.

Charge-off – The creditor's acknowledgment that they do not anticipate collecting on a debt. The creditor writes off the debt, however, the debt remains valid and subject to debt collection.

Closed-End Credit – A loan or type of credit that must be paid off in full by the end of the term. Real estate and car loans are two common examples. Repayment includes all interest and finance charges.

Closing Date – The last day of your billing cycle.

Cosign – The act of signing a credit agreement with another person who agrees to share the debt with you, and assume responsibility for the debt if you default (or vice versa).

Cosigned Account – A credit account that you have signed with another person who agrees to share the debt with you, and assume responsibility for the debt if you default (or vice versa).

Cosigner – An individual who signs a loan or credit agreement with you, and therefore agrees to share the debt with you and assume responsibility for the debt if you default (or vice versa).

Collateral – Property or another asset offered by the borrower to the lender in order to receive a loan. The lender can seize the collateral if the borrower defaults on the loan.

Collateral Estoppel – Also known as issue preclusion. Prevents consumers from relitigating an issue that was resolved in a previous lawsuit—even if the issue at hand refers to a separate claim.

Collection Account – A delinquent account transferred to a debt-collecting organization that seeks payment on behalf of the creditor.

Collection Agency – An organization seeking payment from delinquent borrowers on behalf of the creditor. Delinquent borrowers are often responsible for covering the costs of working with a collection agency. Collection agencies may also request that the credit bureaus add a "collection account" notation to your credit report, which will lower your credit score.

Common Law – Law derived from ancient customs and judicial precedent. Different from statutory law, which is written by legislatures.

Compensating Factors – The borrower's strengths and weaknesses based on their credit history and financial situation. Lenders use compensating factors to evaluate the borrower's creditworthiness. Perhaps the borrower has extensive cash reserves now, but defaulted on a loan several years ago. The former may compensate for the latter.

Consolidation Loan – A loan taken out to consolidate your bills into a single payment. By combining your debts, you can enjoy a lower interest rate and other benefits.

Consumer – An individual who purchases economic goods and services for personal use rather than production or resale.

Consumer Credit Counseling Services – Creditor-funded non-profit organizations that offer consumers advice on debt repayment, budgeting, and other strategies relating to credit.
Consumer Financial Protection Bureau - The Consumer Financial Protection Bureau, or CFPB, is a federal agency charged with being a watchdog for consumer financial products, such as credit repair, debt settlement, credit cards, payday loans, mortgages and student loans. Approved as part of the massive Wall Street reform bill signed by President Obama in July 2010, the agency officially launched in July 2011.

Convenience Check – A blank or transfer check offered when you open a new account. The check is meant to transfer your debt from your old card to your new one.

Copy Charge – A fee card issuers charge for copying and handling. Card issuers are required to give you copies of all the documents relating to your account, but they reserve the right to impose a small fee for this service.

Counterclaim – The defendant's claim opposing the plaintiff's claim in a pending lawsuit.

CRA (Community Reinvestment Act) – Encourages banks to meet the housing and credit needs of the communities where they operate.

Cramdown – Also known as lien striping. In bankruptcy proceedings, the court's imposition of a reorganization plan despite any objections from creditors.

Credit – Deferred payment when making a purchase, based on the promise of paying the full amount plus interest at a later date.

Credit Bureau – Also known as a credit reporting agency. Entities that keep consumers' credit reports on file, and provide copies to card issuers, lenders, and hiring managers on request. Equifax, Experian, and TransUnion are the three main credit bureaus in the United States.

Credit Card – A payment card used to borrow funds or make purchases on credit, based on your agreement to pay the issuer back and cover any additional charges and fees listed in the cardholder agreement.

Credit Card Accountability, Responsibility and Disclosure Act of 2009 – Signed into law on May 22, 2009, the federal act limits when credit card interest rates can be increased on existing balances, requires 45 days' advance notice of significant changes in credit card terms and gives consumers at least 21 days to pay their monthly bills. The bulk of the provisions took effect Feb. 22, 2010. It is also known as the Credit CARD Act of 2009.

Credit Check – An inquiry from a lender or employer to confirm a consumer's credit history .

Credit Counseling – Professional advice on debt management and the responsible use of credit, provided by certified credit counselors. Also known as Consumer Credit Counseling Service (CCCS)

Credit Dispute – To request an investigation of information on a credit report, typically due to an inaccuracy.

Credit File – A collection of information maintained or provided by a credit agency, also known as a credit report.

Credit Freeze – A service available to consumers through the credit agencies which consumers lock down/freeze their credit, preventing new accounts from being opened. It is a useful tool in cases where identity theft has been detected or is suspected. The credit bureaus may charge fees for establishing credit freezes unless identity theft has occurred. They also charge for "thawing" the credit freeze, should a consumer decide to open a new account.

Credit Grantor – Also known as your credit issuer. An entity that grants you credit based on the information on your credit report.

Credit History – A report detailing your history using credit. Addresses the likelihood you will pay future credit accounts on time based on your past activity.

Credit Limit – The maximum amount of credit your financial institution has extended to you—the highest amount of money you can charge on your credit account each month.

Credit Ratings – An assessment of a prospective borrower's creditworthiness with regard to specific financial obligations. Credit ratings apply to businesses and government entities, while credit scores apply to individual consumers. In the credit rating system, 1" is positive and "0" means there isn't enough information on the potential debtor. Ratings "2" through "9" point to negative activity. Similarly, "R" indicates a revolving account, "I" indicates an individual account, and "M" indicates a mortgage account.

Credit Repair Cloud – The world's first cloud-based credit repair software and CRM which powers most of America's credit repair industry.

CROA / Credit Repair Organizations Act – A federal law passed in 1996 by Bill Clinton. It requires companies operating as credit repair agencies to have written contracts detailing the scope and cost of their services to clients. The law prohibits companies from collecting money until after they have performed the services they are offering and also bans companies and consumers from making false statements to credit reporting agencies about negative credit information. In addition, consumers have the right to cancel the contract with a credit repair agency if they do so within three days of signing the documents. All contracts must include a disclosure outlining the consumers' rights among other rules.

Credit Report – A detailed summary of an individual's credit history. Credit reporting agencies keep consumers' credit reports on file and submit them to potential creditors on request. Lenders use them to determine whether prospective debtors are creditworthy.

Credit Reporting Agency – Also known as a credit bureau. Entities that keep consumers' credit reports on file, and provide copies to card issuers, lenders, and hiring managers on request. Equifax, Experian, and TransUnion are the three main credit reporting agencies in the United States.

Credit Risk – A consumer's risk of defaulting on a debt by not making the necessary payments on a loan or credit card bill.

CSO – An acronym for Credit Service Organization - any organization that provides credit repair or credit restoration services.

Credit Score – A statistically-based number that speaks to the consumer's credit report and overall credit history. Credit scores convey how likely borrowers are to repay future debts.

Credit Scoring System – A system that helps determine whether a potential borrower should be extended credit. The FICO scoring system is the most common credit scoring system, wherein scores range from 300 to 850. (Higher scores indicate better credit.)

Credit Time Clock – The maximum time items can legally appear on a credit report. Also known as the Statute of Limitations on Credit Reporting.

Credit Union – A member-owned financial cooperative. Members pool their money by buying shares in the cooperative, and take advantage of financial services that are offered through the organization. Credit unions are typically smaller than banks, and appeal to specific geographic areas, interests, and groups.

Credit Utilization - Also known as "credit utilization ratio" which is used in the calculation of credit scores. It compares the amount of credit being used to the total credit available to the borrower. Having a low ratio has a positive impact on credit scores. Corey says you should keep that ratio as low as possible, both overall, and on each card. The ratio is also known as a balance-to-limit ratio, or credit-available-to-credit-used ratio.

Creditor – An individual or entity to whom the debtor owes money.

Creditworthiness – The consumer's risk of defaulting on future debts, based on their past borrowing activity and behavior with credit.

D

Daily Periodic Rate – Your daily interest rate. The daily expression of your annual percentage rate (APR) can be calculated by dividing your APR by either 360 or 365 (depending on the card issuer).

Debit Card – A bank-issued card wherein purchases are transferred from your checking account.

Debt – Money that is owed to an individual or entity.

Debt Consolidation – The combination of multiple loans or credit cards with a new, single loan offering a lower monthly interest rate and payment, or a longer repayment period. In the context of credit card debt, this often involves a balance transfer from several high-interest cards to a single lower interest card.

Debt Negotiation – The process of negotiating new terms or balance with creditors. It is often used as a synonym for debt settlement.

Debt Settlement – The practice of negotiating and paying a lump sum to settle a debt for less than the full amount. Debt settlement/negotiating companies typically offer to negotiate with creditors on your behalf, and a favorite tactic is to withhold payments from creditors to force a deal, a practice that severely damages the credit score of debtors.

Debt Time Clock – The maximum time parties involved have to initiate legal proceedings. Also known as the statute of limitation on debt collection.

Debt Validation – Also sometimes known as debt verification. The consumer's right to dispute a debt per the Fair Debt Collection Practices Act (FDCPA), by asking the creditor to share information on any collection or charged-off accounts in their name. Collectors that do not validate these accounts are not permitted to disclose the debt to credit reporting agencies. Debt validation is considered a formal investigation.

Debtor – Also known as a borrower. An individual or entity that owes a certain amount of money.

Deed in Lieu – The process wherein the borrower gives the title to the lender in order to satisfy a loan in default and avoid foreclosure.

Default – Failure to fulfill a credit obligation, or meet the terms of a credit agreement.

Defendant – An individual or entity accused or sued in a court of law.

Deferred Payment – A loan agreement wherein the borrower has been granted permission to make payments at a future date, or over an extended period of time. Be wary of skip-a-month payment plans, where interest must be paid on the months you skip.

Delinquent – An overdue account after the debtor has failed to make the minimum payment by the agreed-upon date. Since creditors typically work on a monthly cycle, accounts are often considered 30 or 60 days past due.

Discount – A deduction from the standard cost of something, offered to those who pay promptly, or who pay the full amount in advance.

Dismissal with Prejudice – Generally speaking, the dismissal of a case based on merit, wherein the plaintiff cannot file a lawsuit on the same grounds. In bankruptcy, the dismissal of a case by forbidding the debtor from filing an additional bankruptcy until a certain amount of time has passed.

Dispute – A situation wherein the consumer questions the validity of their credit card bill. Consumers may dispute charges for any number of reasons: unauthorized or excessive charges, for instance, or the merchant's failure to deliver goods purchased on the card. While you do not need to pay the disputed charges while the investigation is underway, you are still responsible for paying the rest of your bill. Also known as a Dispute Letter.

Docket – A calendar of upcoming court cases featuring information on the nature and status of each one.

Due Date – The day by which your credit card bill must be paid. Consumers who make late payments will incur late fees.

E

E-Oscar – An automated system that enables Data Furnishers, and Credit Reporting Agencies to create and respond to consumer credit history disputes.

ECOA (Equal Credit Opportunity Act) – A federal law prohibiting lenders from discriminating against prospective borrowers based on age, income level, marital status, race, religion, or gender.

Effective Date – The date at which the card issuer activates your card, or implement new terms for the card.

EQ – Indicates Equifax, one of the three main credit reporting agencies in the United States.

Equifax – Reports and maintains consumers' credit data. One of the three main credit reporting agencies in the United States.

Equitable – Impartial and just, conforming to basic human rights.

Escalated Information Request – A federal law granting consumers the right to access the information creditors have on their accounts. Creditors must fully disclose the information should the consumer to whom it pertains request it. Investigative in nature, the law may help to improve the consumer's credit after a dispute has failed.

Estoppel – A group of legal doctrines precluding a person from stating something that contradicts a prior action or statement they have made. Individuals cannot speak in opposition to their own actions.

Eviction Action – Also referred to as a forcible entry and detainer or unlawful detainer action. A court action allowing the entitled individual or entity to seize the premises.

EX – Indicates Experian, one of the three main credit reporting agencies in the United States.

Experian – Reports and maintains consumers' credit data. One of the three main credit reporting agencies in the United States.

F

FACTA - The Fair and Accurate Credit Transactions Act (FACTA) is a U.S. resolution passed in 2003 that is aimed at enhancing protections for identity theft. The FACTA created standards for the handling of consumer information, enhancing privacy and accuracy. The act gives individuals free access to their credit reports and is an amendment to the Fair Credit Reporting Act.

Fair Isaac Company – Creators of the FICO score, or the most common credit scoring system lenders use to determine consumers' credit risk.

FCRA (Fair Credit Reporting Act) – A federal law passed in 1970 to regulate consumer credit by promoting fairness and accuracy. Grants consumers the right to access any data credit reporting agencies have filed on them, and to dispute false information. Ensures information that is negative but accurate will disappear after a certain period of time. Also promotes privacy by detailing the specific reasons for which lenders and other parties may request copies of consumers' credit reports, and by limiting their access to these reports.

FDCPA (Fair Debt Collection Practices Act) – A federal law ensuring consumer protection against deception and abuse from collectors.

FED (Forcible Entry and Detainer) – Also known as an eviction action. A court action allowing the entitled individual or entity to seize the premises.

FICO Score – One of the most widely used credit scores used by lenders, calculated and sold by Fair Isaac Corporation.

Federal Reserve System – Also known as the Federal Reserve, or "the Fed." The central bank of the United States, responsible for governing money and credit. The system ensures a stable and secure federal banking system, and oversees matters such as interest rates and the distribution of cash to local banks.

FHLMC (Federal Home Loan Mortgage Corporation) – Also known as Freddie Mac. A public government-sponsored entity created in 1970 to keep a stable supply of money flowing to mortgage lenders in the United States.

Finance Charge – The cost of borrowing money, or the amount the consumer must pay to receive credit.

Finance Company – A company that grants consumer loans, most often to those who are not eligible for credit through mainstream channels such as a credit union or bank. Since finance companies typically welcome consumers with lower credit, they tend to charge higher interest rates.

Fixed Expenses – Costs such as a mortgage payment that are the same each month.

Fixed Rate – An extension of credit where a set interest rate is applied to the principal. The interest rain remains static through the fixed-rate part of the loan.

FNMA (Federal National Mortgage Association) – Also known as Fannie Mae. A government-sponsored corporation founded in 1938 and designed to strengthen the secondary mortgage market.

Foreclosure – A legal action terminating the buyer's rights to the mortgaged property and taking the property into possession when the borrower defaults on their mortgage payments.

Free Credit Report – Per the Fair Credit Reporting Act (FCRA), consumers are entitled to one free copy of their credit report every 12 months from each of the three credit bureaus (Equifax, Experian, and TransUnion).

FTC (Federal Trade Commission) – A government agency responsible for enforcing the Fair Credit Reporting Act (FCRA). The FTC prevents fraud, deceptive behavior, and unjust business practices, and offers consumers tools to protect themselves against these practices.

Furnisher – Also known as "data furnisher" is an entity that reports information about consumers to consumer reporting agencies, which may include credit bureaus, tenant screening companies, check verification services and medical information services. Furnishers are typically creditors, lenders and collection agencies but may include other entities.

G

Garnishment – A court order indicating that money or property (most often the debtor's wages) can be seized to satisfy a debt owed to a creditor.

GNMA (Government National Mortgage Association) – Also known as Ginne Mae. An agency of the United States Housing and Urban Development (HUD) created in 1968. Promotes homeownership by allowing lenders to get better costs for their loans in the secondary market, and therefore helping to reduce costs for buyers.

Goods and Services Dispute – An attempt to rectify a problem with goods or services purchased on a credit card. Depending on the outcome of the dispute, you may not have to pay the full amount owed.

Goodwill Negotiations – Typically involve accounts that are only mildly negative. A situation in which the borrower encourages the lender to accept past-due payments after considering the greater context of the situation. Also known as a goodwill intervention or goodwill letter.

Grace Period – An interval of time during which consumers can pay what they owe in full without incurring any finance charges.

Graduated Payment Mortgage – A fixed-rate mortgage featuring terms that include a gradual increase of the payment amount over time. This type of loan offers low initial monthly payments and typically includes negative amortization—payments that fail to cover the interest due, with the remaining amount added to the principal.

Gross Income – Earnings before deductions and taxes are taken out. In addition to your salary or business profits, your gross income may include alimony, child support, retirement benefits, and rental income.

H

Hard Inquiry – An inquiry in which a lender requests a copy of your credit report after you applied for credit or a loan with them. A hard inquiry will help the creditor evaluate your credit risk. Too many inquiries in the span of six months may affect your credit score.

HIPAA - An acronym that stands for the Health Insurance Portability and Accountability Act, a US law designed to provide privacy standards to protect patients' medical records and other health information provided to health plans, doctors, hospitals and other health care providers.

Holder in Due Course – Protects the purchaser of debt by granting them the right to receive debt payments.

Home Equity Loan – A lump-sum loan with a fixed interest rate. Based on the market value of the home, after subtracting the amount still owed on the property.

HUD (Department of Housing and Urban Development) – A government agency working to create affordable housing opportunities in the United States. HUD's mission is to create inclusive housing communities, meet the needs of consumers from all backgrounds, and strengthen the economy.

Since 1965, the Federal Housing Administration (FHA) has been a part of HUD.

I

Identity Theft – One person's criminal impersonation of another consumer online, by mail, in person, or over the phone—most often by unlawfully gathering other consumers' personal information, such as their social security or bank account number.

IN PERSONA – A court action made against a person and their property.

IN REM – A court action made against a person's property rather than their personal liabilities.

Inaccurate – Incorrect or erroneous, untrue.

Inquiry – A request for a copy of a consumer's credit report to evaluate their creditworthiness. Inquiries take place on submission of every credit application to determine whether a prospective borrower should be extended credit. Excessive inquiries within a six-month period may affect the borrower's credit score.

Installment Account – Accounts with a fixed number of payments over the designated time frame. Personal and car loans are common examples. Installment accounts do not need to be paid in full each month; rather, the same amount will be paid each month until the account is paid off.

Installment Credit – Credit with a fixed number of payments. A component of credit that indicates whether you can maintain the payment amount over time.

Interest – A percentage of the total money borrowed that the debtor must pay in exchange for using the credit.

J

Joint Account – A credit account shared by two or more individuals. All parties are liable for payments on the account.

Judgment – A public record or court decision regarding a person's liabilities in terms of the debt they owe. Court judgments may be featured on the debtor's credit report.

Jurisdiction – The power of the court to make legal decisions pertaining to a consumer or business, and to oversee specific matters relating to the case.

K

L

Late Payment – Past-due credit or loan payments, or payments made after the due date. Late payments damage consumers' credit.

Lease – A written contract in which one party grants another use of land, property, or services for a specific time period.

Liability – The cardholder's responsibility for the charges on their account. Charges may include purchases, finance charges, and interest. If the consumer grants another person permission to use their card, the approved cardholder is still liable for any charges incurred. The details surrounding cardholder liability are listed in your agreement.

Lien – An individual or entity's right to satisfy a debt by holding another person's property until the debtor pays.

Lien Waiver – An official document releasing the debtor from obligations once the full debt has been paid. Contractors and suppliers often issue lien waivers to confirm they have received the full payment and no longer have lien rights to the owner's property.

Line of Credit – A specific amount of credit granted to the borrower. Lines of credit may be secured against an asset to ensure repayment.

Long-Arm Statute – The jurisdiction a state court has over out-of-state defendants who have an adequate connection to the state.

M

Merged Credit Report – A credit report featuring information compiled from all three credit bureaus: Equifax, Experian, and TransUnion.

Minimum Payment – The minimum amount owed to your card issuer each month. Making the minimum payment is ideal for those who cannot afford to pay the full amount they owe, although doing so consistently may result in substantial interest charges.

Misleading – Giving the wrong impression, deceiving.

Monthly Periodic Rate – Your monthly interest rate. The monthly expression of your annual percentage rate, which can be calculated by dividing your APR by 12.

Mortgage – A legal agreement in which the creditor lends the borrower money in exchange for taking the title to the borrower's property as security until the debt is satisfied. The borrower must also make interest payments to the creditor.

Mortgage Insurance – An insurance policy that protects creditors against losses from mortgage defaults. Buyers making a down payment of less than 20% of the total price of the home must typically purchase mortgage insurance.

Mortgage Insurance Premium (MIP) – The cost of mortgage insurance used in Federal Housing Administration (FHA) loans. The FHA will either charge an upfront MIP at closing, or they will assess it annually in a total of 12 installments.

Mortgage Qualifying Ratio – A debt-to-income and housing-expense-to-income ratio mortgage lenders use to determine the borrower's creditworthiness. Most often, the buyer's monthly mortgage payment should not exceed 28% of their monthly income.

Mortgagee – The lender in a mortgage, or the entity on the receiving end of the buyer's mortgage payments—usually a bank.

Mortgagor – The borrower in a mortgage, or the individual with a mortgage on their property—usually a homeowner.

N

Needs – The items needed for basic human survival (i.e., food, clothing, and shelter).

Negative Amortization – An increase in the principal of a loan as a result of the borrower making payments that do not cover the interest owed. By adding any interest owed to the principal, the borrower will ultimately pay the lender more money.

Net Income – The amount of money you receive in your paycheck after adjusting the total for taxes and other deductions.

O

Open 30-Day Account – A credit account in which the consumer must pay back everything they have borrowed at the end of the month—that is, the full balance.

Open-End Credit – Also known as revolving credit or charge card. A loan the borrower is only permitted to use for purchases up to a certain limit. The amount owed must be paid before the due date.

Open-End Lease – A lease in which the consumer must make what is called a balloon payment at the end of the lease agreement. The balloon payment amount is determined by calculating the difference between the asset's residual value (the value at the end of the lease) and its fair market value (the selling price).

Opting Out – You are under no obligation to participate in creditors' pre approved or pre screen offers. To "opt out," simply request that the credit bureaus remove your name from their marketing lists.

Other Charges – Charges posted on your bill such as late payment fees or annual membership fees.

Over-the-Limit Fee – Also known as an over-credit-limit fee. A fee incurred when your balance exceeds your credit limit, meant to deter you from charging more than your credit limit allows. Note that federal law forbids card issuers from charging over-the-limit fees unless you have given your express permission.

Overdraft Agreement – A contract allowing cardholders to continue writing checks when their account reaches zero, without being charged a returned-check fee. Either the financial institution agrees to cover checks that would otherwise bounce, or you can link your credit card to your checking account.

Overdraft Checking Account – A checking account linked to the consumer's credit card so they can write checks for more money than they have in the account. While you will likely pay interest and finance charges on the overdraft, you will not incur returned-check fees.

P – R

Partial Payment – A payment consisting of less than the full amount owed to the creditor. Not all lenders accept partial payments.

Past Due – Your account is past due when you fail to make at least the minimum payment by the due date.

Payment Due Date – The date each month by which payments are due on borrowed money. Creditors who receive late payments typically charge a late fee and/or additional interest. While some lenders may offer a grace period, the borrower is still liable for making timely payments.

Periodic Rate – Your annual percentage rate (APR) expressed over a shorter amount of time—typically a month or a day.

Permissible Purposes – Under the Fair Credit Reporting Act (FCRA), consumers have the right to privacy with regard to their credit standing. Section 604 of the FCRA states that to obtain a copy of a person's credit report, the individual or entity inquiring must have an approved purpose.

Personal Line of Credit – The highest amount of money a consumer can owe based on their financial information and credit history.

Personal Loan – A loan extended based on the borrower's financial information and credit history.

Piggybacking – Piggybacking is the act of attempting to improve your credit score or rating by becoming an authorized user OR joint account holder on someone else's credit card. By doing this, the authorized user or joint account holder inherits benefits of the primary account holder's good credit. It is most often used by parents with their children or with spouses. For piggybacking to work, the "good credit" person must add the "bad credit" or "no credit" person as an authorized user or joint account holder, not the other way around. Due to an explosion in the "tradeline for sale" industry - scoring model companies have made changes to scoring models have placed less or no weight on the authorized user unless the primary is a spouse or family member.

PIN – An identifying number banks or other entities grant to consumers to ensure transactions are authorized. Approved cardholders must select a PIN code and learn it by heart for use at points of purchase and ATMs.

PITI – An acronym for a mortgage payment consisting of principal, interest, taxes, and insurance.

Plaintiff – An individual or entity bringing a case against another individual or entity in a court of law.

Pleadings – The early stage of a lawsuit wherein the parties file formal documents detailing their claims and defenses.

Points – An origination fee the lender charges the borrower at the beginning of a loan. Each point represents 1% of the face value of the loan. Points are different than—and must be paid in addition to—interest.

Post Date – The month, day, and year a transaction is posted by the card issuer to your account. The post date is sometimes identical to the transaction date—that is, the day the transaction was made—but typically one to three days later.

Predatory Lending – A corrupt practice in which lenders impose unfair terms on a borrower. Issuing a mortgage loan to someone who cannot afford to repay it, and therefore stripping the buyer of equity, is one example. Another example is the collection of unreasonably high interest charges, points, and fees with no justification for doing so.

Predictive Variables – Items that help determine consumers' future credit behavior—for instance, their "probability of default." These variables play a role in the credit-scoring formula.

Prepayment Penalty – A charge certain lenders collect when borrowers pay off a loan early—before the end of the term or the specific time detailed in the agreement. Lenders who impose prepayment penalties aim to regulate what the borrower can pay off and when.

Prepayment Penalty Mortgage (PPM) – A mortgage clause in which the borrower must pay a prepayment penalty for repaying a significant portion of the mortgage—typically more than 20% of the principal—within a specific timeframe. The penalty is either based on the remaining balance or on several months' interest.

Previous Balance – The amount of money still owed at the beginning of a new billing cycle, based on the charges accrued at the end of the previous month.

Primary User – The individual whose name is on the credit card, and who is therefore legally responsible for any charges.

Prime Rate – Varies based on the rate determined by the Federal Reserve. The lowest interest rate banks are willing to issue, typically reserved for their best customers.

Principal – The initial loan amount, or the total outstanding balance excluding interest and fees.

Private Mortgage Insurance (PMI) – Protects the lender in the event that the borrower defaults on their mortgage payments. Refer to the term "Mortgage Insurance" for more information.

Promotional – An interest rate available for a limited time. Upon expiration, a higher rate—that is, the ongoing rate—will be added to your balance.

Promotional Inquiry – A soft credit inquiry in which creditors pre approved consumers for a loan or credit card. Since creditors do not make lending decisions in response to promotional inquiries—they simply pre approved consumers for an offer—consumers' credit scores are not affected.

Proof of Claim – A document signed by the creditor in bankruptcy court detailing the amount of money the debtor owed from the time of the bankruptcy filing.

Public Record – Consumer information pulled from court records by a credit bureau. Accessible to the public on request. This information may refer to liens, judgments, or bankruptcy proceedings.

Quitclaim Deed – A title transfer designed to shift interest in real estate property. The current title holder—called the grantor—transfers their interest in the property to the recipient, or grantee.

Rebate/Enhancement Cards – Offer partial refunds or "cash back" based on how much you charge on the card each year. Interest charges may negate the value of the rebate or enhancement card, depending on the card issuer. Enhancement cards come with additional benefits such as frequent-flyer miles.

Redeem – Paying off a mortgage, including any late payments, while a foreclosure suit is underway. By redeeming the mortgage, the buyer can avoid foreclosure.

Renegotiable-Rate Mortgage – Also known as a flexible-rate or rollover mortgage. Monthly payments stay consistent for three to five years, and are then renegotiated until the loan is fully paid off.

Repossession – The borrower's surrender of a possession after defaulting on payments. Repossession can be forced or voluntary.

Res Judicata – Also known as claim preclusion. Indicates that once a court has made a decision on a claim, the parties cannot raise another action on the same claim. The term is Latin for "a matter already judged."

Revolving Account – A credit account in which the consumer, after making the minimum monthly payment, can defer payment on the remaining balance. Deferred payments result in service and interest charges.

Revolving Credit – Credit that consumers can use repeatedly up to a certain limit (that is, if payments are made on time). The amount of credit available, along with the balance and minimum payment amount will fluctuate based on the payments and transactions made to the account.

Risk-Based Pricing – A popular pricing structure among creditors. Credit is extended based on the consumer's creditworthiness. A borrower deemed less likely to default will receive a lower interest rate.

S

Secure Electronic Transaction (SET) Protocol – A communications protocol for making credit card transactions over insecure networks like the internet. Per SET protocol, encryption technology enables secure electronic transactions in compliance with industry standards.

Secured Credit Card – A credit card backed—or "secured"—by the borrower's savings account. Secured credit cards present minimal risk to creditors. The funds in the borrower's savings account serve as collateral, and help creditors determine the borrower's credit limit.

Secured Loan – A loan in which the borrower offers an asset such as a car or real estate as collateral.

Security Interest – A legal claim on the assets the borrower has provided as collateral. These assets can be seized and sold to satisfy the debt if the borrower defaults on their loan.

Seller's Points – A lump sum paid by the seller to the buyer's lender in order to decrease the cost of the loan. Seller's points are common in real estate. One point is typically 1% of the loan amount.

Service Charge – A finance charge imposed for a service relating to the use of your card.

Service of Process – The distribution of court documents to the party to a lawsuit in order to exercise jurisdiction in a court of law.

Sheriff's Sale – Also known as a distressed public property auction or judicial sale. The auction where a property in foreclosure is offered for sale by a sheriff—under the authority of the court—to satisfy a debt.

Smart Card – An electronic prepaid cash card typically exchanged at face value. Smart cards are available at most banks.

Soft Inquiry – An inquiry in which a lender requests a copy of your credit report with no effect on your credit rating. Your free annual credit report is considered a soft inquiry, as are promotional inquiries and your existing creditors checking up on your activity.

S.O.L. – An acronym for Statute of Limitations.

Stall Letter – Also known as stall tactic or stall response, this is when a credit bureau or furnisher responds to a dispute by refusing to comply for various reasons. Generally a stall response is sent to discourage either a consumer or a credit repair company from continuing their quest to repair credit. There are 3 primary types of stall responses. Suspicious request, frivolous request and insufficient identification.

Statement – A monthly bill detailing your outstanding balance, payments, purchases, interest, and other charges. Submitted by your credit card issuer to keep you informed of your account activity.

Statement Date – The date your statement is created, with interest charges included in the balance.

Status – The current state of your accounts as described on your credit report. Includes the account type and where the account stands in terms of payments owed or due.

Statute of Limitations – Also known as S.O.L: The amount of time parties can initiate legal proceedings or report information. See Debt Time Clock.

Stay – A court order where a specific action can no longer be taken until the court lifts the order, or until circumstances change.

Stored-Value Card – A prepaid card containing stored value that you can spend on transactions. Often issued to consumers who cannot open deposit accounts (i.e., a checking account).

Subprime – Credit or loan products for consumers with a poor credit history. Subprime loans have a higher credit risk, and therefore feature higher interest rates and fees. The approval process and lending terms are typically more lenient than alternative loans.

Summary Judgment – A judgment conveying that no factual issues are left to be tried, and jurisdiction can be exercised over a claim without going to trial.

Subscriber – A company that pays to report data to a credit bureau.

Summons – A notice in a lawsuit requiring a party's presence in court, with judgment rendered for failing to appear.

Surcharge – Also known as a checkout fee. A charge imposed by a merchant to consumers who pay with a credit card rather than cash. Certain states have credit card surcharge restrictions.

T

Tax Lien – A last resort imposed on the property of a debtor who owes back taxes. The lien is filed by a taxing authority against the debtor's assets.

Terms – The specifics regarding the loan agreement, including the interest rate and the time it will take for the debtor to satisfy the debt.

Three C's – The three primary areas lenders use to determine creditworthiness: capacity, collateral, and credit.

TILA (Truth in Lending Act) – Details important information on credit terms that can help consumers make sound credit decisions and protect themselves against unfair or inaccurate billing practices. Amended by the Fair Credit Billing Act (FCBA) in 1974.

Tradeline – Credit account records given to the credit bureaus. Tradelines may appear on the consumer's credit report. Mortgages and lines of credit are two examples.

TransUnion – Reports and maintains consumers' credit data. One of the three main credit reporting agencies in the United States.

Transaction Date – The date a transaction is made. Note that the transaction may not be posted until one to three days after the transaction date. Refer to the term "Post Date" for more information.

Tri-Merge – All three credit reports from Transunion, Equifax and Experian compiled information into one report and taking the duplicate information and merging it as one account.

Transaction Fee – A fee the cardholder incurs when specific transactions take place (i.e., consumers are often charged a transaction fee for cash advances).

TU – Indicates TransUnion, one of the three main credit reporting agencies in the United States.

U

U-CCC (Uniform Consumer Credit Code) – A statute detailing the standards of credit transactions, with the aim of providing protection for consumers.

UCC (Uniform Commercial Code) – The laws relating to commercial transactions, designed to regulate financial contracts.

Unsecured Loan – Also known as a signature loan. A loan based solely on the borrower's promise to satisfy the debt, without savings or collateral offered as security. Limits are typically lower than in secured loans, and interest rates higher.

Unused Credit – The credit available before you reach your limit, or the unused part of an open line of credit (i.e., a credit card or loan).

Unverifiable – Unable to be verified, or that which cannot be proven accurate.

V

VA Loan (Department of Veterans Affairs) – The Department of Veterans Affairs is a federal agency that coordinates loans and other benefits for American veterans and their dependents. The VA Loan is a popular home-mortgage option among these individuals.

VantageScore - A credit score product launched in March 2006 by the three major credit bureaus (Equifax, Experian and TransUnion) as a competitor product to the FICO score. Similar to a FICO score, a VantageScore is a three digit numeric value that assesses a borrower's credit risk.

Variable Expenses – Expenses that are not fixed, and therefore vary each month. Gas and grocery transactions are common examples.

Variable Rate – An interest rate that may vary over time due to changing economic conditions. Different than a fixed-rate loan, which does not change as the loan progresses. The fluctuations in a variable-rate loan affect your payment amount each time a change is made.

W – Z

Wants – That which human beings desire for comfort, convenience, and status rather than survival.

Warranty Deed – A document that protects the buyer by pledging that the grantor—the current homeowner, or seller—does not have any liens or mortgages against the property at the time the title is transferred.

Wraparound – Known as a "wrap" for short. A form of secondary financing in which the seller lends the buyer the difference between the purchase price of the property and the existing loan. The idea is that the buyer's subsequent payments will cover both loans. Wraparound loans appeal to buyers who are not eligible for conventional mortgages or financing.

Writ of Assistance – A court-issued written order that a law enforcement official (i.e., a tax collector or sheriff) complete a specific task.

Writ of Execution – A court order granting a law enforcement official the authority to seize the defendant's assets in order to satisfy a debt after the court has issued a judgment.

Other

"A" Loan – A loan offered exclusively to consumers with good credit. "A" loans offer ideal terms and a low interest rate.

"B" or "C" Loan – A loan more readily available to consumers with poor credit. "B" and "C" loans do not offer ideal terms—borrowers will likely have to pay additional fees—and typically feature a higher interest rate.

2nd Mortgage or "Secondary" Mortgage – A loan taken out after the first mortgage—a lien on a property that is subordinate to an existing mortgage or trust. Buyers may take out a second mortgage to consolidate debt, finance a home improvement project, or for other reasons.